Getting It Together

Organising the Reading-Writing Classroom

Getting It Together

Organising the Reading-Writing Classroom

Edited by

Walter McVitty
and
the Publications Committee:
   Vivienne Nicoll
   John Vaughan
   Lyn Wilkie

Distributed in the U.S.A.
by
HEINEMANN EDUCATIONAL BOOKS, INC.
70 Court Street
Portsmouth, New Hampshire 03801

Primary English Teaching Association

Contents

Statement of Principles 1
    John Steinle

Scheduling the Classroom Day.................. 5
    Peter Sloan & David Whitehead

Organising Space and Materials................ 21
    Hazel Brown

Grouping for Personalised Classroom Learning ... 31
    Len Unsworth

Contracting 49
    Alma Fleet

Peer Tutoring................................. 65
    Staff at Knox Grammar School

Parents, Teachers, Children and the Literacy
Curriculum................................... 77
    Max Kemp

Team Teaching................................ 87
    Mary Mannison

Learning Centres and Literacy Development 101
    Len Unsworth

Index 120

Statement of Principles

JOHN STEINLE

Director-General of Education
South Australia

SOMEWHERE IN THE CLUTTER OF MY MIND is a story I read about an incident at Winnetka when Carlton Washburn was introducing the idea of individual progression. A teacher in her last year of dedicated service was toiling away, long after the school day had finished, preparing the enormous amount of material that was required for her next day's lessons. Washburn entered the room and was appalled to see her, weary and wet-eyed. His immediate reaction was to take the pen from her hand and to send her home with the injunction that she was to disregard all his requests about individual instruction. She had taught long and successfully in the conventional mode and it was no time for her to change her style in the twilight of her career.

I am not sure if the facts are correct but the story does serve to make the point that teaching is an art and not a science and that it is an intensely personal matter. It is about people influencing the development of other people in a manner which is enjoyable and comfortable to both. There is no one single formula for doing it.

selves and sought to assist teachers in different ways from the hierarchical approaches which had been used for so long. Now younger people, variously called "consultants" or "advisers", who were essentially outstanding teachers taken out of classrooms for a limited period, were given the task of assisting their colleagues. They did this by demonstrating their own techniques, drawing on conventional wisdom and educational research, and influencing not only the classroom practice of individuals but also curriculum and classroom design. They also arranged in-service conferences aimed at the true professional development of teachers.

It was these people who demonstrated in a very practical way that the professional development of teachers should not be left to any one source. Rather, the successful development of teachers is multi-faceted and requires a pooling of knowledge from many sources.

It was the advisory teachers, too, who brought home to their colleagues the fact that not only should they devise a style which was comfortable for them, but that they should critically examine a vast range of approaches and techniques in order to discover a teaching style which suited them. Professional development programs were planned to provide opportunities for the study of current theories and research and innovative practices. The experience could then be applied to individual classrooms. Teachers increasingly took advantage of opportunities to observe other successful teachers and also children, in order to understand them singly and in groups, to understand their own strengths and weaknesses, and finally to understand what primary education is endeavouring to do for children. This supplemented the undergraduate studies which provided the knowledge and skills necessary to enter the field and to provide a base for future learning.

Obviously such observation does not need to be conducted at first hand. As with all learning this can be done by books and films and discussion. In the case of observing children, however, nothing surpasses the opportunities presented to a vigilant and observant teacher who is supervising children at play in the school yard, or on school camps, as well as in the classroom.

Understanding oneself is perhaps the most difficult thing to do. This requires honesty, a willingness to seek and heed criticism and to be prepared to change one's attitudes and practices. Certainly the task is made easier in the presence of competent and perceptive colleagues and by reading the thoughts of great thinkers and practitioners. Can teachers read Vickers Bell's book *On Learning the English Tongue* without being stirred to improve their story telling skills? One of the pleasing aspects of this kind of self examination is the discovery of skills and abilities in oneself. How often do people who are shy and withdrawn with adults find that they have great skills in communicating with children?

An essential part of the process of developing a teaching style is to develop a social classroom organisation. This necessarily reflects the wide range of approaches we have seen already. There are those who prefer the flexible, open approach which allows for and even encourages educational serendipity. There are others who choose the rigorous, highly structured approach, with its emphasis upon predictability and formality. Even more teachers choose a position in the middle and endeavour to provide opportunities to take advantages of both approaches to meet the needs of the moment.

Both approaches have their adherents who defend their practices with missionary zeal, and both can work well if they are genuine, consistent and in keeping with the general milieu of the school. It is important therefore not only to explain one's position to colleagues, parents and children but also to accept that others may not agree with the style.

Thus, while we have examined the dichotomies in primary education, we have recognised the areas of agreement between the various groups who espouse different approaches to the teaching of children. These agreed practices are both numerous and important. They are especially significant in the matter of

Scheduling the Classroom Day

PETER SLOAN
DAVID WHITEHEAD

Western Australian College of Advanced Education
Mount Lawley

In this chapter, scheduling the school day is presented as an important area of teacher planning, which requires decisions to be made according to a number of interacting variables. Stress is laid on devising schedules which allow the children to develop independence in learning and to take responsibility for some or most of the activities which they will encounter. Independence and responsibility are major skills in successful development, but they are not achieved quickly, nor will they be achieved totally in the primary school. Teachers must be prepared to accept approximations towards these goals and to provide the models needed to gain the insights required. Without the opportunity to apply these skills in the learning situation at every level of the school they will not be learned at all.

The various ways of scheduling the day presented in this chapter have been selected because they are flexible enough to allow the teacher to achieve the delicate balance between teacher guidance and children's independence and responsibility, which maximises and characterises effective learning. Although a child centred approach is emphasised, it is conceded that a totally child centred approach is not always workable, nor desirable. The skilful teacher is the teacher who can make learning appear to be learner directed and who can provide experiences in independence and responsibility.

The schedules discussed and presented here are aimed at facilitating the development of an active, positive and purposeful classroom experience for both learner and teacher.

Learning principles

The scheduling of the classroom day must take into account the principles of learning, i.e. those factors which maximise the acquisition and retention of information. If the daily schedule does not accord with these principles which underpin all learning, little or no learning will result. These principles are briefly stated in the following section of this chapter.

(a) *Attention*

Without the learner attending, learning cannot take place. Only when the learner is alert and focused on the task can learning begin. Sometimes attention to the learning experiences, by the learners, is minimised by how long they have been required to attend to one task, and the type of attention required, e.g. visual concentration, listening concentration etc.

It is easier to acquire information and to retain it longer when attention is maximised.

Scheduling the classroom day must take into account the importance of attention as a major factor in effective learning.

Implications

Attention span varies with age. The attention span of younger children is significantly lower than that of older children. Therefore the time spent *attending* in any one mode (e.g. listening, observing, doing) must take the attention span of children into account.

Thus, it is suggested that teachers vary the kinds of activities in a learning experience, according to the ages of the children and the nature of the task. The following figure (Figure 1) provides a summary of the generally accepted functional attention spans at three levels of the primary school.

It is important to ensure that learning activities (e.g., discovery, instruction and application) are not prolonged beyond the attention span limits. One way to overcome the attention span variable is to adopt a cyclic approach to the scheduling

Attention span in minutes	YEAR LEVELS		
	1-3	4-6	7-9
Low	5-9	10-14	15-30
High	8-12	13-24	25-40

Figure 1. Average Attention Span in Primary School Children. *(After* Gagne 1976)

of activities. In Years 1-3, for example, nine to twelve minutes of exploratory work with concrete materials may be followed by up to twelve minutes of instruction (discussion, demonstration etc.) and then up to twelve minutes of application. Activities will increase the children's attention to the task.

(b) *Meaningfulness*

If what is to be learned is not meaningful (i.e., sensible *and* relative to the learner), he/she cannot learn. The acquisition and retention of information is facilitated if what is to be learned is meaningful. Generally this means that the item to be learned must relate to the previous experiences of the learner. Often, in the primary school, this means relating the new learning to concrete sensory experiences (i.e., looking, hearing, tasting, seeing, touching and smelling).

Implications

Ensuring that new learning is meaningful requires reasonable periods of time. Since it is no use teaching without meaning, consideration must be given in scheduling the day to provide blocks of time sufficient for these meaningful links to be made. The following suggestions for increasing meaningfulness in learning situations have implications for how daily schedules are arranged.

Other principles and conditions

The above principles of learning provide the basic rationale for decision-making regarding scheduling of the classroom day. There are, however, other important considerations which must be taken into account and, in scheduling the classroom day, the teacher must make provision for them.

(a) *Classroom climate*

The daily schedule must foster a happy, business-like and positive climate in which both the children and the teacher can feel comfortable. The work-day of children and teachers can become quite stressful if too much is demanded or impossible deadlines are set for the completion of work.

The classroom effective environment is made more positive through a flexible time schedule which caters for emergent needs and provides for the juxtapositioning of ''light'' and ''heavy'' periods of involvement, application and practice.

(b) *Learning rates and learning styles*

Not all children learn at the same rate, nor do they learn in the same way. Learning rate is governed by many variables such as age, prior experience, intelligence, self-concept, as well as the nature and demand of the task. Learning rates change from activity to activity and are greatly influenced by the learner's attitude towards the task. Learning styles vary in the same way. After a few weeks at school, children get into routines which they find effective. The scheduling of the day must provide for a variety of teaching styles to be used by the teacher, as a means of meeting the differing needs of the children in this dimension.

(c) *Nature of the class*

Consideration must be given to the nature of the class when drawing up daily classroom schedules. Schedules for younger children must reflect the active nature of younger children and their limited capacity to gain and retain large amounts of information in a short time period. Much care must be taken at the lower levels to avoid fatigue, which comes easily if the learning modes are not varied frequently (see *Attention* above).

The *socio-cultural background* of the class is important in many ways, for it influences the effective selection of learning activities, the background knowledge of the learner and the attitudes of the learner towards what is being learned. As a result, some activities will require a longer time in one class than they will in another. In some classrooms much more social learning is required as a pre-requisite to more formal learning. Time allocations are thereby significantly affected.

(d) *Independent work*

All children need to develop independence as learners. A major goal of the teacher from the very beginning of school must be to work towards making the children independent. Not enough attention was given to this goal in the past. Independence comes from understanding the processes, i.e. having the strategies for learning internalised and from having a major responsibility for the learning experiences.

Learners cannot become independent learners/thinkers without the chances needed to develop that independence. Children's growing into independence requires teachers to be less concerned with the drilling of content knowledge. Teachers need to be flexible enough to facilitate the children's attempts and to accept their approximations towards a goal, as they occur.

In terms of scheduling the classroom day, a teacher who is fostering children's independence will arrange a quite different sequence of activities and time allocations from the teacher whose sole purpose is the learning and retention of knowledge (the ''facts'').

Meeting the criteria

The criteria discussed in this section may seem to be impossible to meet but, in the actual creation of the daily schedule, many of the criteria may be met without too much difficulty. Some of the criteria presented above are, however, more difficult to reconcile in every respect. Generally, the criteria discussed here are best catered for in open, flexible arrangements. In the following section, various approaches to scheduling the classroom day will be presented and discussed, with these established criteria in mind.

Approaches to scheduling the day

There are many approaches to the effective use of time in the classroom day. The scheduling of any one day in the classroom must be seen in context because few teachers consider only one day in isolation. Thus is it appropriate to look at the scheduling of classroom activities over a number of days, although our concern here is with the daily schedule.

In some of the examples which follow, weekly schedules are presented because they allow a better appreciation of how the criteria can be met using larger blocks of time and the juxtaposition of components, some of which would not occur daily.

(a) *Contract approaches*

The most open and flexible approach to scheduling the day is the **contract** approach. The contract approach requires the child and the teacher to enter into an agreement about what work will be completed and when. The contract is usually formulated in some way, the most general way being the construction of a timetable indicating the content being covered and the time. Such a contract can be made between an individual child and the teacher, or a group of children and the teacher.

Advantages

The advantage of the contract approach is that it makes provision for:

● individual rates and styles of learning;
● a great deal of learner responsibility for deciding the what and when of the curriculum;
● independent work (i.e. since every contract may be different);
● children working at different levels, without the differences being too apparent;
● time for conferencing (specific times for conferencing may be built into the contract).

In addition, one of the main benefits of this approach is the positive attitude of most children towards this kind of scheduling. When first setting up a contract system, teachers are advised to begin slowly by making only some areas of the curriculum open to contract. In addition, teachers need to train, guide and help the children to develop a contract.

Because children will need guidance, some teachers have found it more appropriate to begin with **group contracts.** In this application, the class is divided into groups of six (six is the best operational size) and, each day or at the beginning of the week, the group plans its activities and work for the contractable areas of the curriculum.

To assist children, teachers should write, on the blackboard, the areas to be covered in the week, so that the groups will know the actual content to be covered and be able to glance through it in order to plan their schedule. In doing this, the teacher can also indicate fixed times when he/she wishes to work with the whole class and when a group must have a conference about a topic. The following example (Figure 2) illustrates a teacher's listing of content, from which each group formulates its own schedule. (Note: The same principles apply to individual contracts.)

(b) *Priorities list approach*

Just as the contract approach is an "open" approach which provides much flexibility, so is the *priorities list* approach to scheduling. In this approach, a teacher ranks in order of importance the task goals for the day. For example, a teacher of a Year 6 class has arranged the following priorities for a day's teaching from a list of tasks or activities to be done (see Figure 4).

Underlying assumptions

There are various assumptions which underpin the "priorities list" approach (PLA). Some of the basic assumptions are related to philosophical orientation and others to practical considerations in meeting the needs of children and teachers. Briefly stated, these assumptions are that:

- Schools attempt to do too much in a day and, in so doing, fragment learning by stopping activities when they have not completely served their purpose and before there has been a chance for children to comprehend fully and practise learning. By listing in priority order those things which are to be covered each day without rigid time constraints, this fragmentation can be overcome.
- The priorities list approach (PLA) is less complex than other approaches and therefore simpler to use and less stressful on teachers. That is, *the teacher just works through the list.* When one task is completed for the day to the mutual benefit of children and teacher, the next task is begun. What is not completed in a day is rescheduled for the next day.
- The PLA reflects real life. One job is completed before another begins.
- Over a period of time, say 5-10 days, the proportions of time allocated to various curriculum areas are met as the teacher has in mind the need for a balanced curriculum.
- The approach is very flexible in that it allows for themes to be selected and those activities which genuinely relate to it followed up in the most appropriate order and according

Class Year 5	Teacher	Mrs K. Smith
School _____		Date 24/10/85

Time Spent	Subject/ Topic	Notes	Comments
	1. Oral Language Daily Programme	Discuss latest news on topic of interest.	
	2. Mathematics — Introduction to X'n of fractions	Book 5, p.16-25. Matching activity. Conference — Joan and Mark.	
	3. Phys. Ed.	Cards 46 & 18.	
	4. Reading	Group: 1. DSR SF Level 15 2. Language Reconstruction 3. Individualised reading 4. "	
	5. Art	**Appreciation** — Examine prints on use of line. **Perspective** — Using lines to capture mood.	
	6. Writing	Revising drafts of report on class trip. Conference with Alan, Bill, Mary and Sue.	

Figure 4. Day Pad — Priorities List

TIME	BLOCKS	CURRICULUM	SUGGESTIONS FOR ACTIVITIES
9.00	1. **Language**—exploratory and instructional	Oral language	Discussion of —News —Objects —Interesting events —Listening/speaking games —singing
9.30		**DEVELOPMENTAL ACTIVITIES AND READING**	
		Reading During developmental activities, the teacher works with groups and/or individuals inc. —Language experience —Shared book —Direct silent reading	**Development Activities** —Play with objects, blocks, water, sand, play-dough, construction materials. —Sorting, matching, pairing of beads, buttons, bits and pieces. —Play acting, dressing-up. —Drawing, painting, cutting, pasting. —Talking, telephoning, educational games. —Listening to music, tapes, educational radio. —Shop and house play.
10.30		Recess	
10.45	2. **Mathematics**	Maths	
11.15	3. **Language** enrichment and Production	Uninterrupted Sustained Silent Reading (USSR)	
11.30		Language (Related Language Arts)	Choral Speaking Writing stories, speaking and listening, spelling, printing and handwriting.
12.00		Lunch break	
1.00	4. **Cultural Studies**	Art Music Physical Education Social Studies Reading	Reading to children Nature Walks Various other related activities
2.00	5. **Language** and **Cultural Studies**	Language Social	Performances and sharing, writing and doing.

Figure 5. Blocked Time Approach to Daily Scheduling

General Timetable for Years 1 to 3

Block 1 and Block 5 may be juxtaposed to provide for an out of class experience or some similar learning situation. Figure 5 also shows some breakdown of the blocks into curriculum areas and activities by way of illustration of how the blocks may be used.

Blocked schedules can accommodate a wide range of activities, thus allowing for specific instructional needs to be met in well defined areas of the curriculum (e.g. social science, science, drama and music) which become more academically focused in upper school classes. Figure 6 shows a format in which the morning blocks, where the basic skills are taught, remain the same for each day. However, the afternoon blocks have schedules which vary daily to accommodate specific curriculum areas.

Daily schedules for Year 1

The scheduling of the school day for children in their first year at school requires the teacher to take a more active role in organising the learning experiences. Accordingly, daily schedules for Year 1 classes tend to be more teacher centred in the arrangement of activities. This is not to say that children in Year 1 are not capable of some independent work, nor that they should not have a chance to be independent. It is just an acknowledgement that the capacity of children at this age to sustain long periods of concentration is limited.

Moreover, the beginner needs some predictable structure so that a sense of security is created. For these reasons, schedules in the very early years tend to be teacher directed and the learning activities kept short to retain interest and involvement. Despite these limitations, as already stated, the teacher should, from the very beginning, foster independence by having the children suggest what activities should be scheduled and by having the children become more responsible for initiating work within activities. After a few weeks some children are ready for a little independent work in some areas, e.g. recreational reading, instructive play and some stages in writing.

The following set of schedules reflects the blocking of curriculum time as a means of organising the time in a Year 1 class. It should be noted that, at the earliest stages, activities are scheduled for 20 minute periods. This brief scheduling of activities is a reflection of the principles which underpin the daily schedule applied to this level of the school.

These three schedules give some idea of the pattern of the day but they can easily be adapted to suit other patterns of work.

It should be noted that the length of the school day varies from place to place. We know that children differ in their adjustment to school and that their needs vary from time to time. The conditions operating within the school must also be taken into account as must other factors such as school bus schedules.

With the new entrants to Year 1 there will be no reading groups as such, but, as soon as some children are ready to read in a group with the teacher, it is suggested that the last part of the morning and afternoon be used for this purpose. At this stage it would seem to be of benefit to all concerned for the teacher to allow the less advanced children to indulge in free activities within the classroom. This is greatly facilitated if a teacher aide is available.

Gradually more children will be ready to stay on the full time, but the teacher, by then, will be more able to cope because the more advanced children will be becoming independent.

Learning centres and the daily schedule

There are two types of learning centres:

1. An activity area (*corner*) set-up for work or exploration on a **subject** or **interest** basis and permanently available. Examples of this kind of learning centre are the following activity areas or corners:

Reading	Science	Play
Writing	Construction	Maths
Listening	Art	Home
Drama	Music	Talking

In each of these areas, activities, resources and materials related to each area are stored and displayed or ready for use. The activities are changed frequently and children are often given specific tasks to do in working sessions with the teacher, which must be completed in the relevant area.

2. A special location or display on a particular theme. The theme may be derived from social science, science, a current interest or literature. This type of learning centre, which contains resources, materials and displays, remains in place as long as the theme it supports is being treated.

Learning centres, when organised thoroughly and when the children are shown how to use them, can provide the framework which allows teachers to partially or completely individualise their program. Learning centres provide opportunities for children to practise the skills which they have been taught in instructional situations and, in so doing, provide chances for independent learning and the growth of learner responsibility.

In blocked schedules, where there is considerable time available for many different activities in an area (e.g. language: speaking, listening, reading and writing), learning centres provide opportunities for more than one activity to be pursued at any one time. When used in this way, learning centres provide the basis for what to do with the other children (the children with whom the teacher is not at that moment working).

The organisation of effective learning centres makes blocked and individualised schedules achievable, as well as providing the positive child centred learning outcomes already mentioned.

References

Bennett, N. *Teaching Styles and Pupil Progress*. London, Open Books, 1976.

Blitz, B. *The Open Classroom: making it work*. Boston, Allyn and Bacon, 1973.

Hertsberg, A., and Stone, E. *Schools are for Children*. New York, Schoken Books, 1971.

Holt, J. *What Do I Do on Monday?* New York, Dutton, 1970.

Sloan, P., and Latham, R. *Teaching Reading Is* . . . Melbourne, Nelson, 1981.

Organising Space and Materials

HAZEL BROWN

Balarang Primary School
Oak Flats (N.S.W.)

This chapter begins by looking at the conditions which enable pre-school children to master the oral language of their environment surely and successfully. It then suggests ways of managing resources and space within the classroom to allow for similar "natural" conditions to apply in other areas of language learning, e.g. reading and writing. Written by a practising classroom teacher, it describes her own practices and is, therefore, a personal description of a single (but successful) classroom in action— an extended case-study of one person's approach.

learning. Within this, the language plan itself, the activities and strategies used, the materials provided for use and the physical layout of the room have evolved, changing many times, until we have now arrived at a situation where real learning is occurring. By this I mean that learning is individualised totally, each child determining his or her own language activities, working at self-determined rates, progressing and changing when confident to do so.

There has been a positive growth in self-discipline, the ability to organise time, respect for other children, their strengths and limitations, and their need for personal space. Children have imposed upon themselves natural standards that suit their situation.

There are no graded groups or obvious units of comparison. There is co-operative learning, freedom, responsibility and enthusiasm that could never be planned for. Cambourne's conditions provide the structure for this language plan, where the main focus is reading. Literature is the demonstration of good writing, the sources of words and language which children need to become able communicators. It is the centre from which all other language activities naturally flow.

Figure 1 represents the conditions of natural learning and their practical application in the classroom.

Immersion in a literature-based language classroom means, in large part, print resources. It is worth spending time discussing these.

Resources
Print—tools of the trade

The provision of resources suitable for such a plan is arrived at by trial and error. It is essential, however, that adequate and accessible materials are provided: resources that are extensive and comprehensive, because just as the learning environment of the developing infant provided endless examples of speech patterns, so a classroom must extend the scope of language to

Figure 1. Conditions for Natural Learning in the Classroom

the child and provide many examples of the written word. Just as the oral language learner needed saturation in the medium to tease out how the grammar, the sound system and the rules of talk worked, so the written language learner needs thousands of examples of how punctuation, story structure, characters, genre, purposes and a host of other attributes makes written language work.

A teacher therefore must ask:
● Will there be *enough* printed matter to cater to the needs of the class?
● Is the material suited to the *interests* of the children, their age and capabilities?
● Is there a *variety* of materials, especially in terms of "register" and genre?
● Is the *quality* high? (Is it a good demonstration of written language?)
● Will the children get the maximum *use* from the materials made available to them?
● Are the *ground rules* of use known and understood?

Figure 2 summarises the resources aspect of the language plan.

onto overhead transparencies. Children can and will use audio-visual equipment competently and responsibly. Although books are our major print resource in the language classroom, audio-visual equipment can be used to provide children with models of other writers' products.

A cassette player linked to a listening-post provides a ready source of stories. There are many commercially available kits catering for all abilities and ages K-6. They come complete with sets of small books so that children can "read-along" with the taped story.

Teachers can also make up their own sets. Most schools have multiple copies of suitable books, e.g. Dr Seuss series, Mt Gravatt, Rigby, *School Magazine* stories and articles. It doesn't take long to read a story on to tape yourself. Making the recording yourself means that you can add instructions at the end of the tape, e.g.

- *"Rewind the tape and listen again"*
- *"Stop the tape and go to the large table. From the story you have just heard, draw . . . and write words which describe them."*

The overhead projector is an excellent aid to help the teacher demonstrate the processes involved in composing and editing a piece of writing. It is also a useful tool to use in group work. While one group of children can be working with the projector, the teacher is then free to work more closely with other children.

6. *Immerse the room in print*

A literary environment—immersion—should not of course stop with the selection of books. It should extend to the walls, windows, bulletin boards and hanging space in the classroom.

- If a poem or song is treated, letter it on colourful cardboard and display it clearly.
- Science experiments can be written up by a group of children and displayed.
- Social studies work (particularly that which shows all the hallmarks of quality writing) and other well edited and revised work should be hung wherever space allows.
- Stories taken through to publication should be shown to be valued and displayed, either in a class anthology or on a bulletin board.
- Good leads for stories, written by children or gleaned from printed books should hold a prominent place.
- Charts of synonyms, similes, problem words etc. should form part of environmental print.
- When walls and windows are full, use hanging space and create mobiles of print matter.

Environmental print must be of a high standard to help create a stimulating and cheerful room of which children are proud. Such print should have some degree of logical order to it so that a child feels secure and will know where to find appropriate vocabulary in a particular writing situation. Don't take down displays as soon as a unit of work is finished—take down only when new space is required. A child's interest in a topic does not finish when the timetable does; often a child will want to revisit a theme and write and read about it long after a teacher has finished treating it.

Environmental print is especially important for developing readers. To such readers, particularly those children in the lower grades, wall print is as much a reference aid as dictionaries are to senior or more independent children.

7. *Get children to "engage" with print*

How do we make children aware of our print resources? Try the following:

- Take infant grades on "print walks" each morning at the start of language lessons. Read from just one section of your room each day if the room holds lots of exciting print, but make sure the children are aware of where the words are.
- Display books well by:
  —having them arranged in library fashion, i.e. fiction, non-fiction, poetry, magazines etc.;
  —keeping books on a theme or by the one author together;

the young reader to cope with the expository style of writing.

One important thing to keep in mind when gathering resources for a "print-saturated literary environment" is the **time** factor. When learning to talk, a child has unlimited time within which he listens to demonstrations of correct speech. Language time in a classroom is much more defined and therefore the quality of our demonstrations of good writing must be of a high standard—quantity now being replaced by quality. So determine your purposes and objectives and build quality materials to help you achieve these.

Organising space and time

My daily language plan, at the moment, lasts for two hours and is broken up in the following way.

withdraw one parallel group of six so that I can monitor and evaluate progress. At all other times the child makes the decision, selects the activity and determines where the activity will take place.

The first ten minutes of language always requires the children to be together. This whole class focus is a settling time, focusing in on language and literature. Depending on the activity, the class will be seated either on the floor in the library area or at their desks.

Floor space is preferred if I am
● reading part of an on-going serial;
● telling a story;
● "selling" books;
● discussing authors or stories.

Often, after having read a story, the whole class might spend

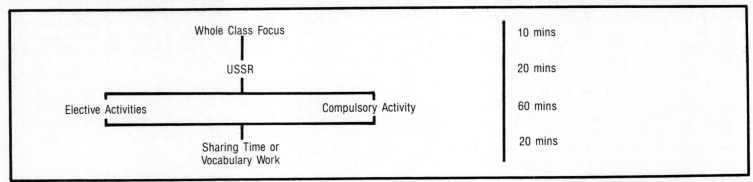

It has been designed in such a way that the children in my class take control and responsibility for their development in reading and in writing, so that language is totally individualised. For this reason my class has taken an active part in the selection of language resources and we have a comprehensive collection of books, magazines, language activities and inviting reading is needed. The only time I as a teacher obviously intervene is during the compulsory activity when, each day, I

the first ten minutes analysing characters or the significant happenings of the tale. This activity requires me to record responses. With senior pupils an efficient way to do this is by having children sit at desks, with teacher working at the chalkboard.

Next, USSR follows for approximately twenty minutes. Seating is self-selected at this time and can take place on seats or on the floor. A comfortable environment in which free

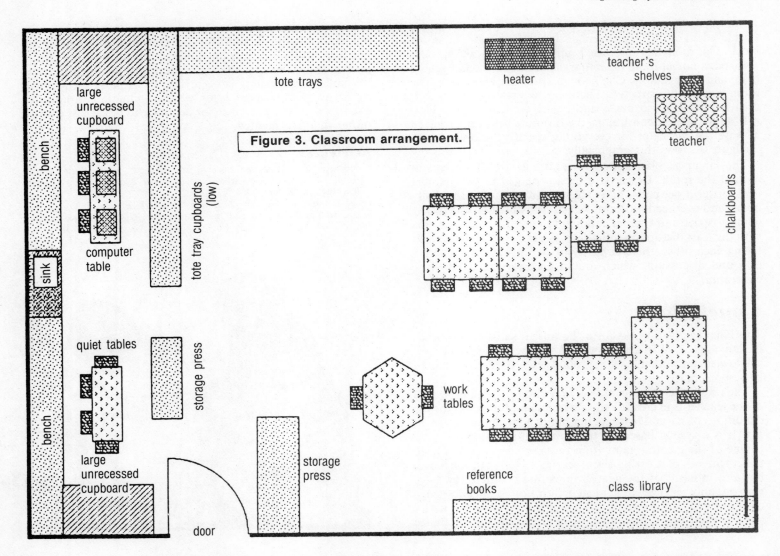

Figure 3. Classroom arrangement.

bench

large
unrecessed
cupboard

computer
table

sink

bench

quiet tables

large
unrecessed
cupboard

tote tray cupboards
(low)

storage press

storage
press

door

tote trays

heater

teacher's
shelves

teacher

work
tables

reference
books

class library

chalkboards

Grouping for Personalised Classroom Learning

LEN UNSWORTH
Macarthur Institute of Higher Education
Milperra (N.S.W.)

The first part of this chapter discusses the theoretical and practical basis for providing personalised learning experiences for all children through appropriate grouping techniques. This is supported by a brief survey of recent research on grouping and the teaching of reading. A practical approach to more flexible within-class grouping is then described and illustrated by a detailed class program based on modern fairy tales. Teachers are encouraged gradually to extend the flexibility of their classroom management beyond this concept of classroom groups so that, through the establishment of more co-operative learning environments, they can maintain a personal and individual response to the developing needs of all children in their schools.

operating on the field.

(Price, W.T. *Introduction to Data Processing*, p. 196.)

All readers of this chapter can, no doubt, say all of the words. All can, like the present writer, give a meaning to each word and yet, like the writer, many readers won't have a clue what this means. One or two people may know very well what this means. All readers of this chapter are of about the same reading ability and yet, for this passage to be of instructional value, the writer would have to organise differential learning tasks, taking into account readers' interest, or lack of it, readers' background knowledge etc.—despite the fact that all are in the same ability group! And yet many classes face such a situation, demonstrated by the "computer" passage, as the norm. All of the children in the same group get the same book, or worse, the same card—and even that would be excusable—but there is no attempt at differential teaching according to the different knowledge and experiences different children within the same group may bring to the task.

If reading and writing occur as an integral part of children's learning throughout the school day, there are many opportunities to extend children's real world experiences through practical work in science, drama, music etc. and to introduce, through oral "contextualised" language, the unfamiliar vocabulary and language structures that are relevant to the reading material naturally associated with such learning experiences. In some schools several classes still have a common period of reading instruction when all children are redistributed on the basis of reading ability, to a different class group which is constituted solely for the reading lesson. These practices do not take account of the nature of the reading process and how reading is developed as a natural part of children's learning. Such practices in ability grouping rest on the rather comfortable, convenient but simplified view of the world which asserts that individual learners can be homogeneously packaged for easy handling. Fortunately, research on grouping and the teaching

of reading has begun to expose some of the dangers inherent in such a view.

Current research
Ability grouping and reading teaching

Two recent publications have dealt with the issue of grouping pupils for reading instruction. The first, edited by Dianne Lapp (1980) and entitled *Making Reading Possible Through Effective Classroom Management*, is oriented to the practical concerns of teachers at the workplace and provides a broad summary of the relevant research. In one article O'Donnell and Moore suggest that the research literature dealing with grouping and organisational plans can be summarised as follows:

1. *Homogeneous grouping has not been demonstrated to be an effective method for raising the reading achievement levels of pupils.*
2. *Ability grouping tends to result in a hardening of the categories, especially among low achieving pupils.*
3. *Interaction among pupils of different attainment levels tends to stimulate less able pupils.*
4. *Criteria for composing groups has to be carefully examined.*
5. *Grouping plans should include analysis of strengths and weaknesses within groups.*

A more comprehensively documented review of the research is provided by Hiebert (1983) entitled "An Examination of Ability Grouping for Reading Instruction" and published in the *Reading Research Quarterly*. It may be useful to cite some of the studies which provide the basis for the general position as represented by O'Donnell and Moore (1980). Hiebert notes that there are very few studies that provide information on how reading group placement influences achievement over and above initial differences in reading achievement. The few studies that do exist, however, seem to support the view that homogeneous grouping is not an effective method for raising reading achievement levels of pupils. A recent International Reading Association *Newsletter* (October, 1982) reported a study dealing with

Hawkins, 1966,67; Pikulski and Kirsch, 1979; Weinstein, 1976). It is beyond the scope of this chapter to give a detailed review of the literature dealing with each of these issues. From the evidence which has been presented it is clear that teachers need to abandon many traditional classroom management practices.

Teachers need to confront current research and theory in an effort to establish sound bases for constructing their own innovative approaches to managing learning environments.

Initiating the change

It is not easy to dismantle conventional approaches to classroom organisation within a school. However, many teachers are making good headway in improving grouping arrangements within their own classrooms. They often start out with the usual three groups, then gradually change. A useful transition is the "group-then-regroup" strategy which I have described elsewhere in a program for a Year 4 class (Unsworth, 1984). The same strategy has been applied to one learning experience for Year 3 pupils. Richard Parker (in press) proposes the following Directed Reading/Listening Activity using *The Big Orange* (Mt Gravatt Reading Series, Level 3):

● *Look at the cover.*
● *What do you think the story might be about? Why?*
● *Let's turn over to the first page and look at the picture. Do you still think the story is going to be about _____? Why? Why not?*
● *Now we're going to read the first page.*
   (The reading could be aloud (by teacher and/or pupils), or silent.)
● *What do you think will happen now?*
   (Again, require children to justify their previous viewpoints.)
   Then read to the end of page 4—repeat procedure.
● *Were we right? Did _____ actually happen? What will happen now? Why?*

Then read to the end of pages 10, 12, 13, 14, 15, using the same sorts of questions.

At the end of the story, comprehension may be expanded by asking such questions (with justification of answers as required) as:
● *Do you think this really happened?*
● *If you had been Ben, what would you have done with the big orange?*
● *If you were the shopkeeper, what would you have done with the big orange?*
● *What else could Mrs Fletcher have done with the big orange?*
● *How would you have felt if you were Jason or one of the footballers?*

Parker then indicates how the "group-then-regroup" strategy would be applied to this activity. First, the following Reading Guide was prepared and the same set of directions was recorded on cassette tape.

READING GUIDE   *THE BIG ORANGE*

1. First of all, look at the cover of the book without opening it. What do you think the story might be about? Why?
2. Now turn over to the first page and look at the picture. Do you want to change your ideas about the story? Why?
3. Read the first page. Before you turn the second page, try to guess what will happen in the next story.
4. Read to the end of page 4. Were you right about the story? What did you read that surprised you? Why? What do you think the author will write about on the next pages?
5. Now read to the end of page 10. Were you right? Were there any surprises? If so, why do you think the author wrote the story that way? What will happen over the page?
6. Read to the end of page 13. Were you right? Were there any surprises this time? How do you think the author will end his story? If some people in the group don't agree, explain why you think your suggestion is the right one.
Decide which ending is best.
7. Tell your teacher that you are ready for a change of groups.

Frequently the groups "rotate" after each groupwork session so that each group experiences the three modes of teacher management, although each group may be involved in quite different learning experiences for any one mode.

Further development in the management of classroom groups is related to a number of important dimensions of teachers' professional growth. These include:

- a continuing desire to seek positive, personal and meaningful relationships with all pupils demonstrated by a thorough knowledge of each pupil's background, interests, abilities, likes and dislikes.
- a commitment to operating in classrooms as a member of an educational team which might include fellow teachers, teacher aides, parents, resource teachers, consultants and other professionals.
- maintaining the currency of their knowledge of the processes of literacy and implications for classroom practice through professional reading, post-graduate study, attendance at conferences, seminars etc.
- understanding the difference between teaching and learning and increasing one's capacity to provide a stimulating and well organised, yet flexible, environment for independent learning.

With these perspectives it is soon realised that one can vary not only the number of groups but also the number of pupils per group.

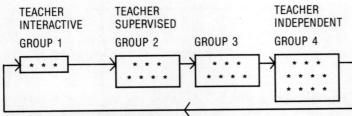

Figure 2. A four group plan.

The groups can then be combined in different ways as suggested in Figure 3.

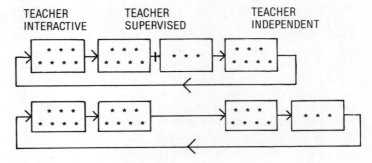

Figure 3. Combining groups.

Not all groups need to experience the various teacher management modes for the same period of time, so the notion of "rotation" is replaced by a more functional distribution of teacher time. This is demonstrated in the following plan for a sequence of groupwork activities with a primary class.

Recycled fairy tales

Only the approach to grouping is discussed here but this must be seen as just one part of an overall program through which the teacher might focus on *fairy tales* to further develop in children's reading and writing:

- an appreciation of plot, setting, characterisation, theme and different writing styles,
- an awareness of role stereotyping,
- an understanding of the way text characteristics can signal an interpretive oral reading of the story.

The classroom activities preceding this groupwork activity might include children sharing with the class their favourite fairy tales, bringing the books from home, discussing whether these

Pick-a-path

This activity, derived from the "choose your own adventure" concept, is included in the Teachers' Resource Book for the recently published "extension" phase of the Young Australia Reading Materials (Baxter et al., 1985). The children are presented with a multiple path outline for a fairy story (Figure 5).

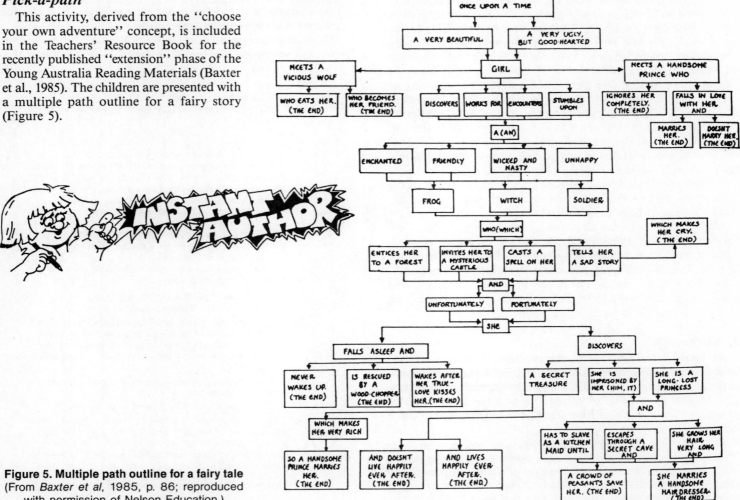

Figure 5. Multiple path outline for a fairy tale
(From *Baxter et al*, 1985, p. 86; reproduced with permission of Nelson Education.)

may, for a purpose such as the presentation of a book review, a play, or some other sharing activity, need to prepare the reading so that the presentation is expressive and stimulating to listen to. It is therefore important to teach children how to rehearse for such reading. They should be shown how to score their scripts, using symbols or devices of their own choice.

A groupwork schedule

The organisational plan for this groupwork is summarised in Figure 7. The children in each group are informed in advance about what they will be doing each session by a classroom group guide.

SESSION	TEACHER INTERACTIVE	TEACHER SUPERVISED	TEACHER INDEPENDENT
1	Pick/Path		Plot Profile Writing Oral Reading
2	Plot Profile	Pick/Path	Writing Oral Reading
3	Oral Reading	Pick/Path	Writing Plot Profile
4	Writing	Oral Reading Plot Profile	Pick/Path
5	Oral Reading Plot Profile	Writing	Pick/Path
6	Pick/Path	Oral Reading Plot Profile Writing	

Figure 7. Groupwork schedule

Session 1

During this session the majority of pupils will be involved primarily in independent silent reading.

Plot Profile Group

Pupils browse among the variety of fairy tales which now populate the "reading corner". These include favourites brought in by the children from home, copies of the tales read aloud by the teacher, the modern fairy tales listed above and perhaps also foreign language versions of fairy tales.

Writing Group

This group will also browse in the reading corner with the object of collecting jottings that may help in composing their own modern fairy tale. The teacher may provide some suggestions, e.g. "Space Age Fairy Tales" and stimulating displays such as a "magic mirror", posters of castles, dungeons, frogs etc.

Oral Reading Group

A listening post will be used to allow these children to hear a dramatic reading of one of the lesser-known fairy tales. At the conclusion of the reading the teacher has recorded some comments and questions asking the children to reflect on *how* the story was read. The tape informs children that such reading takes a good deal of practice and preparation and invites the children to listen to a second story, this time following a "scored" script used by the reader in rehearsing for this reading.

Pick-a-Path Group

During this initial session the children in this group work with the teacher, who introduces them to the peg board format of the multiple path outline as shown in Figure 5. They first experiment with selection of different story lines by removing or reversing the unwanted cards. Then they add cards to increase the range of possible stories. After this they work with the teacher to reassemble new cards, wool and tees to map the basic

Session 5

Plot Profile Group and Oral Reading Group

Both groups work with the teacher. New sub-groups are formed on the basis of children who are working on the same story. Children share their insights into the story, derived separately from plot profiles and prepared oral reading. The teacher elicits from the children their understanding of the way in which language is used in characterisation, the creation of atmosphere and the patterning of plot development.

Writing Group

Children in this group will be making decisions about proceeding toward publication. Some may already be working on the final "published" version. Others may still be editing and revising their drafts. Those who do not proceed to publication may be exploring alternative modes of expression. These could include scripts for classroom video production, fairy tale limericks etc.

Pick-a-Path Group

Children continue drafting the elaboration of their chosen story path in preparation for sharing with other group members and the teacher in the subsequent session.

Session 6

Pick-a-Path Group

"Writers' Circle"—the children in this group "conference" with the teacher to discuss the various story versions created from the multiple path outline.

Plot Profile Group

Pupils complete the final (public) version of their plot profiles for display to the whole class.

Oral Reading Group

Children record their prepared reading onto cassette tape. This may need to be done in the "hat room", the "wet area", outside, in the reading loft, on the verandah etc.

Writing Group

Some children may be proceeding with the production of the published version of their modern fairy tale. Others may explore the production of promotional publicity material for their friends' stories. These might include "classified ads" relating to the story, skill profiles of characters, report cards on certain characters etc. (Johnson and Louis, 1985).

Regrouping

The products of these activities can then become the basis for a three session rotational groupwork plan which allows all of the children to share and enjoy the work of their peers.

SESSION	TEACHER INTERACTIVE	TEACHER SUPERVISED	TEACHER INDEPENDENT	
	(A) Plot Profile	(B) Pick/Path	(C) Oral Reading	(D) Writing Modern Tale
7	C	D	A	B
8	B	A	D	C
9	D	C	B	A

Figure 8. Regrouping plan

Over the three sessions, as each group comes to the teacher, the children first of all create with the teacher a simple plot profile for a well-known fairy tale, e.g. *The Three Little Pigs*. The teacher then distributes copies of the pupil-constructed profiles produced by the previous Plot Profile Group, which have been cut up so that the incident summaries (in their component pieces) are separated from the graphic representation of plot tension. The children reassemble these (rereading the text where necessary) and compare them with the intact versions of their peers' work.

Maxine Murphy, who works in a team teaching situation with about 100 five year olds at Conifer Grove School in Auckland, New Zealand:

> I prepare a chart for each day's activities. It tells each group the four or five activities I expect them to do that day. In the 45 minute period, they know they can choose to spend as much time as they need at any one activity. Generally, they follow the activities I suggest, but they know that they don't have to do everything if they don't want to.
>
> It's important, of course, that I know who has done what, so that I can guide the children if they get into a rut. At the end of every Language Workshop I ask the children to indicate which activities they did and I quickly note their names beside the activity. I find that sometimes the children like the freedom and security of staying with one activity for a while, especially if they are involved in writing an interesting piece. This does not worry me, as long as it doesn't go on for too long. (*Turbill and Butler*, 1984, pp. 26-7)

Rather than indicating when certain groups will undertake experiences which are primarily teacher interactive, teacher supervised or teacher independent, Maxine has included the three management modes within the list of choices for each group. She is therefore able to handle the number of children requiring close interaction with her by moving from group to group. The activities undertaken by each child are noted and most of the evaluation is done while the children are working. Cumulative records are updated with each child once per week, and this information is used in negotiating activities to be done in the following sessions.

There are many other approaches to grouping and co-operative learning which are consistent with the views expressed in this chapter, e.g. "adoptive classes", where each child in a Year 5 class "adopts" a partner in a Year 1 class. On a rotational basis a quarter of the Year 5 class visits the Year 1 partners for one session each day to read to them etc. Correspondingly, for other sessions, groups of Year 1 pupils join the Year 5 class to enjoy a play, singing etc. Thus for one session at least each day the teacher has her/his class decreased by twenty-five percent. And this is not to mention the positive benefits to the children of participating in a co-operative learning enterprise with other children and their teachers.

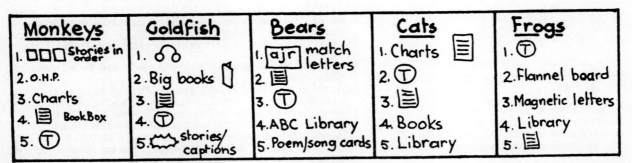

Figure 9. Maxine's daily activities chart
(From *Turbill and Butler*, 1984, p. 27)

McDermott, R. P. *Kids Make Sense; an ethnographic account of the inter-actional management of success and failure in one first grade classroom.* Unpublished doctoral dissertation, Stanford, 1976.

Minard, R. (ed.). *Womenfolk and Fairy Tales.* Boston, Houghton Mifflin, 1975.

Munsch, R. *The Paper Bag Princess.* Toronto, Annick Press, 1980.

O'Donnell, M. P. and Moore, B. "Eliminating common stumbling blocks for organizational change" in Lapp, D. (ed.), *Making Reading Possible Through Effective Classroom Management.* Newark (Delaware), International Reading Association, 1980.

Parker, R. L. *Putting the Guesswork into Reading.* Sydney, Reading Association (in press).

Phelps, E. (ed.). *Tatterhood and Other Tales.* New York, The Feminist Press, 1978.

Pikulski, J. J. and Kirsch, I. S. "Organization for instruction" in Calfee, R. C. and Drum, P. A. (eds), *Compensatory Reading Survey.* Newark (Delaware), International Reading Association, 1979.

Price, W. T. *Introduction to Data Processing.* San Francisco, Rinehart Press, 1972.

Rosenbaum, J. E. "Social implications of educational grouping" in D. C. Berliner (ed.), *Review of Research in Education*, Vol. 8, Washington (D.C.), American Educational Research Association, 1980.

Rosenshine, B. V. and Berliner, D. C. "Academic engaged time" in *British Journal of Teacher Education*, 1978, 4, 3-16.

Sloan, P. and Latham, R. *Teaching Reading Is . . .* Melbourne, Nelson, 1981.

Smith, F. *Understanding Reading* (3rd Edition). New York, Holt, Rinehart and Winston, 1982.

Turbill, J. (ed.). *No Better Way to Teach Writing!* Sydney, Primary English Teaching Association, 1982.

Turbill, J. *Now We Want To Write!* Sydney, Primary English Teaching Association, 1983.

Turbill, J. and Butler, A. *Towards a Reading-Writing Classroom.* Sydney, Primary English Teaching Association, 1984.

Unsworth, L. "Meeting individual needs through flexible within class groupings of pupils" in *The Reading Teacher*, 1984, 38, 298-304.

Walshe, R. D. (ed.). *Donald Graves in Australia: "Children want to write . . .".* Sydney, Primary English Teaching Association, 1981.

Weinstein, R. S. "Reading group membership in first grade: teacher behaviours and pupil experience over time" in *Journal of Educational Psychology*, 1976, 68, 103-116.

Wilson, R. M. *Diagnostic and Remedial Teaching for Classroom and Clinic.* Columbus (Ohio), Charles E. Merrill Publishing Co., 1981.

Williams, J. *The Practical Princess and Other Liberating Fairy Tales.* New York, Parents Magazine Press, 1978.

Contracting

ALMA FLEET

Institute of Early Childhood Studies
Sydney College of Advanced Education

A contract is a written agreement between teacher and learner in which the learner undertakes to complete tasks in a stated time on his or her own initiative. The author suggests some desirable outcomes and outlines the history of contracting and the rationale for it. In this chapter, examples of different contracts are given and there are interviews with teachers who use this system to educational advantage.

bells to tear him away at an appointed hour and chain him pedagogically to another subject and another teacher. Thus treated, the energy of the pupil automatically runs to waste. (p. 16)

The second principle is **co-operation**, with a focus on "real social living" and a sense of community.

In practice, children under twelve years of age physically signed a contract, while older children did not. The curriculum was divided into subject lots; contracts had a month's work stated. Teachers specialised and taught in one of the areas with children from a range of grades attending their lab simultaneously. The student discussed the program with an adviser, agreeing to spend more time earlier in the morning on weaker subjects. During the three hour morning period (9 a.m.-12 noon) children were free to study with anyone else who was in the same lab on a similar task. Children missing several days through illness simply picked up work where they had left off, without being disadvantaged by the pace of an on-going group. Work completed was recorded on a graph, while the teacher maintained a weekly comparison graph of all work being completed by the children in that class.

Subject sharing took place for an hour each day (12 noon-1 p.m.) when the teacher could introduce new material and students could share queries on their assignment. (Different subject each morning: maths, English, history, geography, science. Music, art, movement, cooking, became afternoon subjects.) Parkhurst applied this system in many situations, but saw it as not applicable for children under nine years of age.

Parkhurst emphasised the importance of setting appropriate tasks for the students:

> Few children at any age know instinctively how to work. As the object of the Dalton Plan is primarily to teach them this, the instructor should be careful at the outset not to expect too much. (p. 48)

The tasks should not simply be workbook pages or set readings, but should include statements of purpose, suggestions, guiding questions, experiments, written work and points where

reference to the teacher would be helpful. She suggested that proposed assignments should be posted on a staff board one week before being given to students, so that staff would be informed about what each other expected, unrealistic demands by over-enthusiastic specialists could be toned down by colleagues, and staff could see possibilities for cross-curriculum integration.

The scheme was not intended as a model for use, but as a starting point for others to apply in their own circumstances. Many of the ideas were applied, while others became unrecognisable (e.g. subject specialists with all students doing the same material simultaneously). In England the 12-1 p.m. lessons were not appropriate because of the larger number of core subjects in secondary school, so one full morning and three afternoons were turned over to teacher-led subject instruction. A Leeds headmaster adapted the system to an upper primary school and had contracts set weekly rather than monthly. Subsequent assessment at all levels showed the children's testable achievement to compare with and slightly exceed those in other systems, and characteristics such as "capability, initiative, and power to take responsibility" (p. 176) commendable. Children's opinions were also quoted at length, supporting the system enthusiastically.

Many of the ideas can be adapted and applied usefully in today's schools.

Moving more quickly through the historical development, it can be summarised that such an approach reflected the humanistic orientation of John Dewey and his followers. The late 1960s and early 1970s saw educators such as Herb Kohl, John Holt and Jonathon Kozol agonising about the state of the American school system and calling for alternatives. G.B. Leonard proposed an almost Utopian solution in *Education and Ecstasy*, in which a school open to the community involved children working on their own interests at their own pace. Developing somewhat earlier, the English integrated day system, as described in the Plowden Report and encouraged by the

Figure 1. "Choosing Time" Contract

actual designs are limited only by imagination. Older children could assist in devising their *own* formats. There are also examples of contracts in the literature which can serve as starting points. (Note, for example, several designs in Fleet & Martin, 1984, pp. 60-69.)

The contract shown in Figure 3 could be used with individuals who need to improve a certain skill. Stencils are made and filled in to suit individuals when required. This contract may be useful when conferencing with a child about his/her process writing.

The contract shown in Figure 4 may be used to motivate children to complete their work. When an activity is finished, the child cuts it out and pastes it in the appropriate space on the right.

N.B. The examples shown in Figures 3 and 4 have been adapted from Kaplan (1980).

The teachers speak

What do teachers who are using contracts have to say about them? To give some examples of possibilities to supplement the material, the author selected several interviews. While the explanations are interesting in their entirety, space does not permit full transcription. However, some edited portions should give readers a general feeling of two very different situations, both of which are working well for the teachers and children concerned. These interviews constitute guidelines for two different ways to operate contract programs.

Interview 1:
DOREEN STOKES, *Principal*
Riley Street Infants, Surry Hills, N.S.W.
Year 2, 20 children

As a "teaching mistress", Doreen finds a contract system essential to enable her to fulfil her varying roles:

This is something for them to go on with so I can get on with it. Otherwise they'd all be sitting there waiting for me

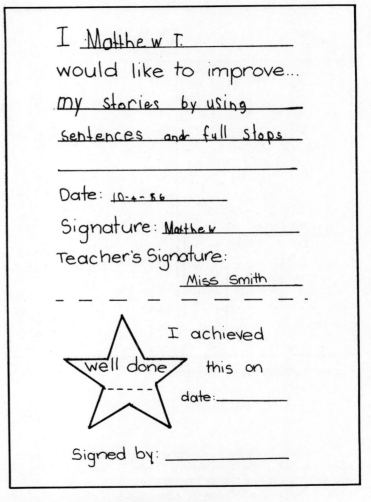

Figure 3. Specific Skills Contract

An interesting contract system is one based on a "Bingo"-type sheet (Figure 5) which is distributed to all children in the class. The contract is used on a daily routine, "around other happenings", the main ones being:

	Mon.	Tues.	Wed.	Thurs.	Fri.
a.m.	Spanish	Library	Scripture	Spanish	
p.m.		Park ESL		ESL	Movement Spanish

TV programs are recorded, to be played back later, at convenient times. During very busy times, like Monday morning, the work which must be completed first is asterisked: *All the other days they realise, of course, they have to get onto the hard core stuff, but they can still do that in any order they like. Parents are also coming in to work with the computer, and the children are often involved with that.*

Specific items on the contract:

- "Meaning card" is done with a partner; better readers are paired with less advanced to read the card and then help them work together.
- When reading a "topic book", the children must find out something they didn't know before.
- If there's a queue at the maths cards, for instance, children go onto something else. Such tasks are initially ability-assigned tasks: *They know their level; they know where they're at, so they get on with it.*
- When reading, children can read to a partner, themselves, or the teacher.
- Number games they choose themselves. Tutor tasks the teacher chooses; children ask when they are ready.
- Craft is set up all the time as an option when other work is finished.
- Children help each other with Spanish from all the words displayed around the room.

- When work has been corrected it goes into a box.

Doreen goes through the new maths material with a small group before the written work is assigned. She is working individually with children or with small groups whenever children are occupied with contracts. Social studies, music and sport are taken with everybody.

How do the children cope?

They're battling. There's very rarely a day that they would get through it all; it's there as an extension. There are nine activities there, which is quite a big task, but everyone always has something to do, even the most able.

I'm finding they get through the Wednesday program very quickly, so I'll have to rethink that. Next term I will be putting in dictionary skills. When I find they're ready for something, I put that in, and I might take out something else. If I find they're able to get through everything, I might introduce a project book for them on any topics they're interested in—to find their own information, which is reading and writing, seeking information and putting it into their own words.

I find that on Thursday they like to get into the story writing straight away. I really don't care if they don't do anything much more than that because the "write a story" covers a writing lesson, spelling, creativity. It covers many things that are far more valuable than doing a sentence kit card or a phonic card.

This is a Year 2 class, but you've also used this system with first class, haven't you?

Yes—then I started with one day—say Wednesday—with a half sheet and three to four tasks. They'd learn to do those tasks in any order in the assigned time period. They need to be able to read and write for this approach so the contracts were introduced gradually, one by one, as the year was going along and the children gained the independence and skills. Then they can jump from one day to a full week's sheet; once they understand it they can go on.

the room and still make it work. *Of course, having laboratories does help! I wouldn't start off with it straight away until I knew the children and their abilities. It has to be a gradual thing, in the right atmosphere, where no one feels threatened.*

Interview 2:

Wenona Junior School
Walker Street, North Sydney, N.S.W.
Family grouped—48 children
JUDI BLAIR (*Head Teacher*)
VANESSA KING
WENDY SHEPHERD

In this team-taught, open-plan infants program, the children are set assignments by the teacher in individual books once a month. The next week's tasks might be written in from mid-week onwards, but the children only complete one week's work at a time.

What are your basic categories?

Judi: Well, there's language, including news and story writing, sounds work—anything related to words, basically. It's not closely categorised at all. I find it's easier for the children if I number them. If they see they have ten assignments, then several days later they can see they have three. The whole idea is that the children budget their times. If they feel they have time to go play, paint, make things during Monday, they can. Most of them like to get their work done and have Friday morning free.

The major categories are language and number. Another is for specific tasks. For instance, I have two children who need extra gross and fine motor activities. We put that down to make sure they're actually doing it and not avoiding it.

How do you start with Kindergarten children who can't yet read?

Judi: They bring their assignment books to us and we ask them to choose activities. Then they go and do the task. When it's finished, we show them where it's written and mark it off. They learn that when something is completed and corrected they can mark it off. Older children help them to find the right books or place in their assignments.

Does it actually start from Day One?

Judi: Yes. The very first day all of them have their assignment books. Those coming back from the previous year know what they're doing and simply carry on. The youngest five in each group are the only ones who have to learn something new.

How many things would be expected for each child?

Judi: For the youngest, by mid-year, about six or seven. Those in the middle tend to vary more, we find. They don't all get through the same amount of work. The older girls would have about ten things.

Is there much work done with, say, pairs of children, or is it mostly individual?

Judi: We've started them reading in pairs. Some of them do their comprehension tasks together. Discussing really helps them understand. Two days a week some of the older children work together as a reading group; they're a bit more responsible and able to organise themselves. They also read to us every day on an individual basis, but that's not written down.

Vanessa: I also do a fair bit of practical maths in twos and threes when I've been teaching a new concept, so that the children get practice before using a workbook. Each week there's a new concept coming in, something being practical from the previous week and something being reviewed from before.

Wendy, from your point of view as a first year teacher who had been briefly introduced to contracts before, how have you found working with them here?

Wendy: Very good. The children need the contracts as a boundary for what they can do; they feel safe within that; they don't feel safe not knowing what's expected of them.

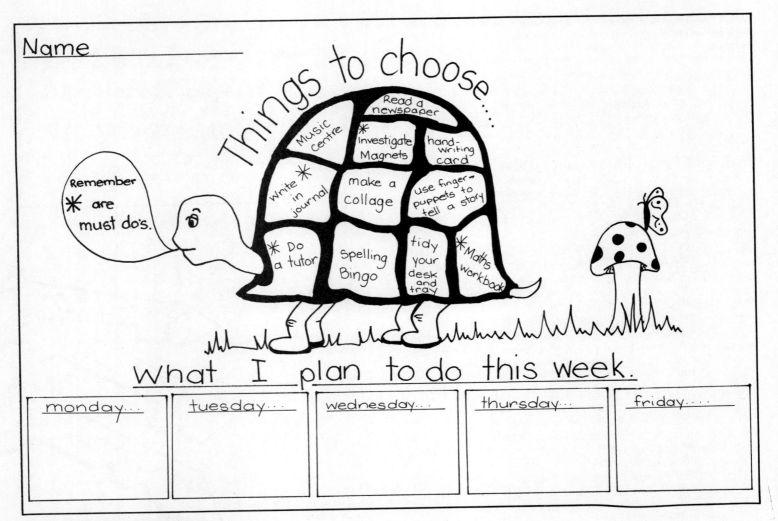

Figure 6. Colour the Turtle

that have to be done are those marked with an asterisk (*). When the child has completed an activity, s/he colours in the appropriate space on the turtle's back.

Another interesting approach is the use of "keychains" (Figure 7). For this method a different coloured key is made for different working areas. After working in an area the child fills out a key and adds it to his/her chain. This enables the child to keep a record of what has been done. It also gives the child a sense of achievement and shows the teacher how the children have used their time.

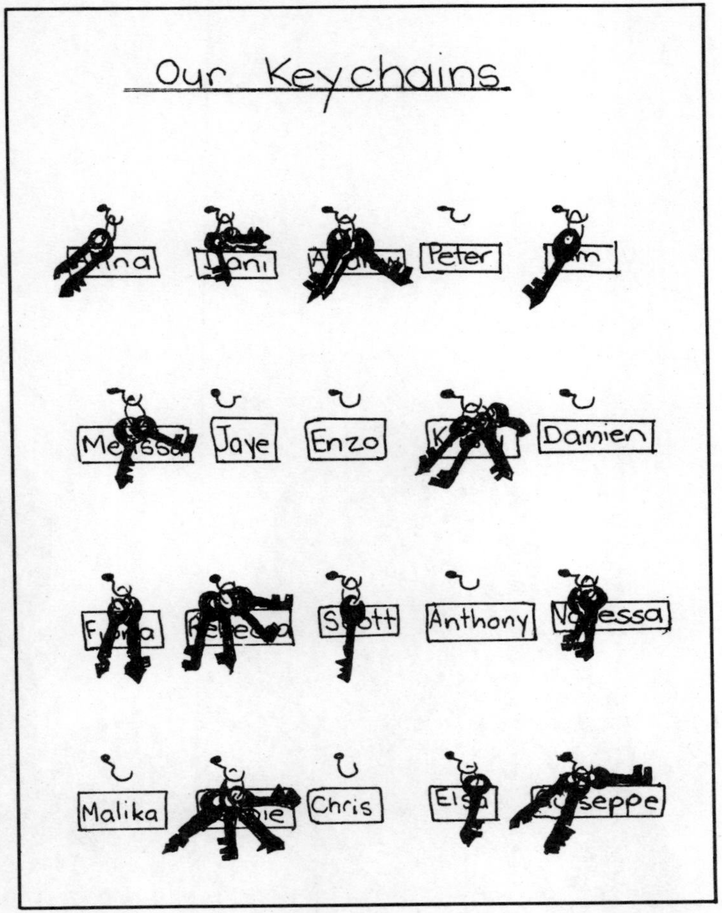

Conclusion

The possibilities with contracting are endless. Here are a few reminders:

- Start *slowly*.
- Teach children how to work *independently* and how to use the relevant *materials*.
- Establish a comfortable (accepting and challenging) *climate* in the room.
- Avoid emphasising *product* to the exclusion of *process*.
- Plan for *small* and *large group* activities as well as *individual* work.
- Give children *concrete experiences* before expecting them to complete worksheet or kit material.
- Analyse each child's *interests, needs and abilities*.
- Monitor children's *physical* whereabouts.
- *Experiment* to discover a system appropriate to your children, yourself and the practicalities of class size and resources.
- *Respect and enjoy the children.*

Implicit in all that has been said here is a belief about learning which echoes Mrs Parkhurst and Professor Nunn in the 1920s but which is very applicable today. Whenever you link your teaching with a philosophy about learning, there is potential for great learner success and teacher satisfaction.

Figure 7. Keychain Contract

Peer Tutoring

PETER C. COOPER
BRIAN R. DAVIES
JEREMY HOLDERNESS
GRAEME A. HUDSON
RICHARD M. PETERSON
ROBYN K. TOPP
ROGER J. TOPP

*Staff at Knox Grammar School,
Sydney (N.S.W.)*

Peer tutoring can be an effective way to influence a child's self-concept. This article describes several classroom co-operative learning activities that allow students to work in teams to achieve a common goal. The article stresses methods of peer teaching that enhance group responsibility and awareness of goals. It emphasises that among the qualities of interaction present in peer learning are the negotiation of teaching and collaborative roles, attention-focusing, showing and pointing and informative messages.

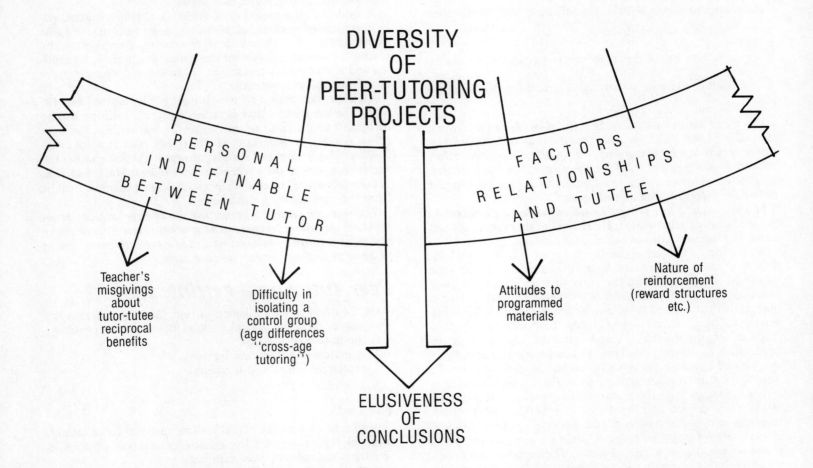

Figure 1. Factors which complicate the research on peer tutoring

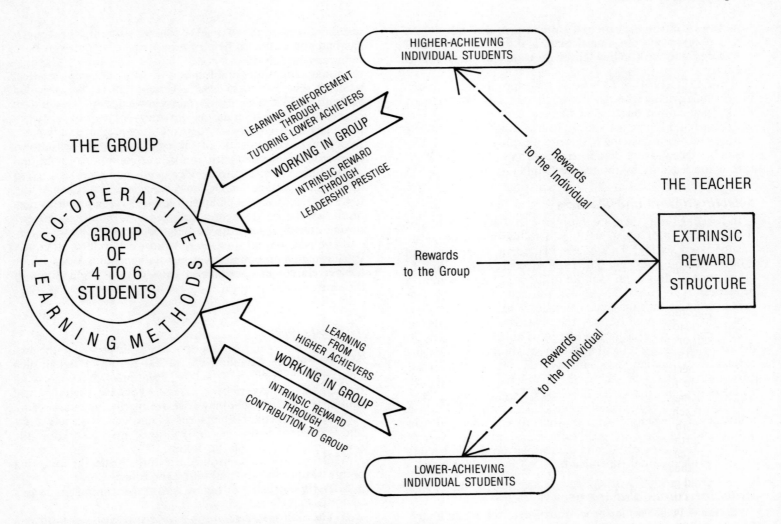

Figure 2. The academic and social benefits of peer tutoring as a group process

Once the role of the tutor has been defined, the structure of the tutoring session needs to be clarified. The following structural elements are advisable, but it must be kept in mind at all times that each element will vary according to class and grade level:

1. Knowing the assignment for the session, and what (if any) stationery, equipment or supplies are needed. The tutor will need to gather these items before the session starts.

2. Tutors need to be aware of suitable responses to their tutees, the types of activities and the correct place to conduct them.

3. After the tutoring session, the tutor is responsible for returning equipment. This is also the time when tutors relay to the teacher information about the progress made during the tutoring session. Whatever the form of the tutor's report (e.g., oral, written) it is necessary to provide some basic guidelines as to the type of information required by the teacher.

Tutoring—theory into practice
Case study 1: Presentation of a science lesson

Individual differences have always been the delight and bane of teachers. Partly in an effort to meet the demands of those differences and provide learning experiences which are stimulating, meaningful and educationally sound (as opposed to dull and repetitious) the following program of peer tutoring was embarked upon.

Task

Tutors, with helpers, were to select an animal, bird, reptile or fish which they would research and present as a lesson to a group of children from each class from Kindergarten to Year 5.

Selection of tutors

Fifteen of the more able members of a Year 6 class were chosen to act as tutors. (These were "more able" only in that they were able to miss some class work without falling behind their peers, who didn't miss any class work.) The children chosen had to demonstrate a degree of self-confidence, since they were to be a model for their peers who, during the exercise, would learn from them how to be a tutor.

The whole exercise was designed to provide the tutors with a chance to be teachers, assume responsibility and improve their academic skills; the trainee tutors (helpers) with the valuable experience of being involved in the process from the grass roots up; the tutees with individual attention and enrichment that they might not otherwise receive.

The teachers were provided with an opportunity to spend more time with those who needed more attention. A valuable experience was thus afforded to all involved.

Matching tutors and trainee tutors

After the initial selection of tutors had been performed, each of the tutors was asked to select one or two "helpers". These helpers were themselves to become tutors at a later date. They were not only to *assist* the tutor in the presentation of the lesson but also to *learn* from the tutor **how to prepare and present** a lesson.

The tutors were encouraged to choose people with whom they felt they could work well. Certainly the playground demonstrates clearly that children playing together in friendship groupings learn their games, songs, jokes, riddles and rhymes quickly. For this reason the tutors were allowed to choose their friends to work with.

Only one restriction was imposed on the choice of helpers by the teachers. The children chosen to be helpers had to be able, like the tutor, to miss some regular class time without detriment to their own progress.

wrote was to include comments on behaviour and responsiveness to the lesson that had been presented. The tutors felt that the learners' enthusiasm for the program was clearly demonstrated in the questions they asked before, during and after the lesson presentation.

Case study 2: Paired reading

This sequence of lessons involved an unstreamed Year 5 class. However, these lessons could also be applied across grades (for example, to achieve greater social interaction within a primary school, as well as improve reading skills).

Tutors and learners were carefully selected according to:
   (i) reading levels, and
   (ii) common interests.

The lessons involved oral reading and discussion. There was a daily fifteen-minute lesson for five weeks.

A week before the sequence of lessons began the tutors met with the teacher and were taught their role. Passages were read and then questioning skills were introduced. The tutors were also given a Tutor's Card (Figure 3) which was to act as a guide when they were involved in peer tutoring.

Each tutor also practised filling in a Lesson Report Card (Figure 4), which was to be completed and returned to the teacher at the completion of each lesson.

The tutors were also coached in correcting errors with sensitivity. All these skills were practised through role-play. After several practice sessions the peer teaching began.

The teacher arranged for a wide range of appropriate reading material to be available at the tutee's level. The tutee selected a book for reading. The tutor and tutee then talked about what attracted the tutee to that book, what he or she anticipated the book was about and whether it reminded him or her of another book. The tutor encouraged the tutee to want to read the book.

The tutor read the first paragraph and then allowed the tutee to read until the tutee signalled that the tutor should take over for another paragraph (the signal generally agreed on was by tapping on the table).

An important aspect of the tutor's technique was to encourage and praise. When an error was made the tutor did not interrupt but, at the conclusion of the paragraph, referred back to the group of words where the error had occurred. It was important for the tutor not to "prompt" when an error occurred. The tutor didn't give the correct word until the learner had had the opportunity to self-correct, or until some contextual clues had failed to elicit the correct word. The tutor made a note on the record card of any words which caused difficulty and could not be decoded.

After about ten minutes of reading, the tutor asked questions which involved locating details and inferring future developments from the story.

The Lesson Report Card was then returned to the teacher.

The teacher's *on-going support* and *monitoring* are essential. The peer-tutoring lesson permits the teacher to move freely between pairs, to teach a specific skill to a pair or group of pairs, or to join a pair to enjoy the reading process. Occasional taping of lessons also permits the teacher to monitor the *use of techniques* and the *degree of involvement* of both tutor and tutee.

It is also important to *acknowledge* the valuable efforts of the tutors, while *praising* the attitude of tutees.

In this case study, peer tutoring was found to enhance greatly the children's sense of achievement. It is valuable, if only as a change from the usual teacher-directed format of daily classroom activities.

LESSON REPORT CARD

STUDENT'S NAME:_____ TUTOR'S NAME:_____

Reading Session	EXPRESSION was			UNDERSTANDING was			WORDS WHICH CAUSED DIFFICULTY were:
	Excellent	Fair	Poor	Excellent	Fair	Poor	
1							
2							
3							
4							
5							
6							
7							
8							
9							
10							

(Signed) Tutor: _____

Student: _____

Figure 4. Lesson Report Card

Parents, Teachers, Children and the Literacy Curriculum

MAX KEMP

Director, Schools and Community Centre
School of Education
Canberra College of Advanced Education

"Parental Involvement" is a term which means many different things to different people. It can mean parents performing menial tasks in order to help classrooms run more efficiently, but it can also mean teachers and parents supporting each other in the educational process. This chaper begins with a review of literature from Australia and Britain pertaining to the involvement of parents as home tutors of literature. The author suggests that recent naturalistic studies of literacy learning challenge the traditional view that literacy teaching is the responsibility of the school alone. He then provides a detailed case study of an innovative program devised and implemented in the Australian Capital Territory. This program has been successful in assisting parents to effectively support their children's literacy development at home.

in particular schools have also been reported, and these too are included in the bibliography.

Literacy learning as a developmental learning

Our professional and almost absolute control of literacy learning and teaching has begun, then, to face quite a challenge. The challenge comes from the accumulating evidence that literacy learning is being made to look much more like a developmental learning than it used to. The controlling, locked-in condition of teaching reading and writing when children are six has been, and still might be, favourable for the majority; but for a considerable number of children it is not. Support for a developmental learning model of literacy comes from a number of recently reported naturalistic studies, listed for interested readers in the bibliography. For instance, some three-year-olds are already beyond experimenting with symbols, and are already approximating to skill through self-initiated and self-monitoring attempts to find meaning and give meaning. They are able to reflect, hypothesise and talk about what they are learning through letters, words, and stories in ways that are characteristic of other developmental learnings. Kindergarten teachers report now on the massive writing experiences which have turned five-year-olds into authors as a consequence of the process writing movement (Graves, 1981) when, a few years ago, such developments were unheard of. In each of these illustrations the home influence is likely to be, or has been, of very powerful proportions. Each is able to rest its case, if that is needed, for teachers and parents to be drawn much closer together than they are in the planning and development of literacy curricula in at least the early levels of schooling.

A parents-as-tutors program

The program described in this chapter came about at a time when concerned primary, secondary and tertiary teachers and Schools Authority administrators in the A.C.T. were considering the functions of remedial teachers within the region. Issues which were explored by this group included those of preventative, surveillance and corrective measures in literacy program evaluation. An A.C.T. Schools Authority policy change had seen a shift from the traditional remedial teaching program in primary schools to a gradual implementation of a resource (or classroom-integrated) teaching procedure for assisting children with literacy difficulties. This decision sparked off a move within the Canberra College of Advanced Education (C.C.A.E.) to prepare the resource teachers in training for developing stronger cohesion in literacy curricula between each neighbourhood school and its parents. As a consequence, a program was developed in the Schools and Community Centre at C.C.A.E. to bring children with special needs and their counsellors, parents, teachers and resource teacher into a stronger "systems" arrangement (Holmes, 1980) which would focus upon training parents as tutors to their own under achieving children.

The aims of the C.C.A.E. Schools and Community Centre program were:

i) to provide parents with a regular, structured program of either individual or group sessions which would enable them to build their own observation, recording and tutorial skills in aspects of literacy, and thereby support their children's literacy development at home; and

ii) to give graduate teachers a set of parent-training experiences which would better fit them to plan and undertake parents-as-tutors programs with parents in their own schools.

Three programs were designed to help meet these aims, and each is described below.

i) *Group training program with parents.*

This program includes ten two-hour workshop sessions, using teaching materials and videotapes of techniques such as listening to reading, using correction strategies during reading aloud, assisting in process writing, helping with spelling, group interactions for mutual support, and parent-

Table B
Projected Model for Parents-as-Tutors
Program in Schools

	Phase 3 Resource Teacher/family follow-up program (as long as needed)	Resource teacher's input
Parent's visits to classroom	**Phase 2** Resource teacher and class teacher/ family support program (two terms)	Class teacher's input
Referral of child from class teacher or counsellor	**Phase 1** Parents' seminars (one term)	Resource teacher's/ counsellor's input

read by reading, and to write and spell by writing. Within the process of children doing these things, teachers or parents may find a structure for helping them to perfect the processes. When the structure is imposed upon learners from outside so that reading, writing and spelling are learned as code manipulations, and hence communication must await the children's learning of the code systems, some children will cope but others will not. Most of the children involved in the program have not coped with teaching which has emphasised code systems, although there are also some who have responded to neither of these curriculum approaches.

Psycholinguistic theory appears to have a growing body of adherents amongst teachers. Within school communities including of course parents, it attracts a wide audience for explaining how reading, writing and spelling problems are caused, sustained, then analysed and described, and finally resolved. It also proposes a sufficient number of "freedoms" within its appropriate assessment and teaching contexts to give parents several alternatives in approach when helping their children at home. These assessment and teaching procedures, however, need to be explained and demonstrated to parents.

Structure and content of the parents-as-tutors seminars

When parents are referred by professional services personnel to the program they are usually told that the C.C.A.E. program is one of a number of options. Interestingly there is a high acceptance rate and this indicates both the strong drive many parents have to gain information about literacy learning and teaching practices, and the commitment which they have to assisting their own children. These opinions are borne out in subsequent interviews with parents, when information is sought from them about, amongst other things, their child's school history (Kemp, 1985, [a] and [b]).

Parents then attend the seminar program for ten sessions spread over fifteen weeks, each session lasting between 1½ and 2 hours.

The contents of the sessions, backed-up by a specially prepared manual and audio and visual tapes, is as follows:

Preliminary Session—Videotape of parent(s) and child working together.

Seminar Session 1
- Introduction.
- The purposes of the program; its history and present functions.
- What participants in the past have told us about themselves, their children and their children's schooling.
- Timetabling for 15 minutes each day.
- The "learning climate" (1).

Seminar Session 2
- Listening to your child reading—our baseline measurements of home teaching.

Post-Program Session
- Videotape of parent[s] and child working together.

Outcomes of the program

There are three basic streams of evaluation of the program as a whole, the children's progress being the first, the parents' learning and actual control of teaching at home being the second, and the supervising teachers' effectiveness as support agencies being the third. Perhaps one should simply say that, if the children learn to read, write and spell more quickly and with longer-lasting effects than would otherwise have been possible, then the program would have fulfilled its intentions. Desirable though such outcomes would obviously be, partial fulfilment or non-fulfilment immediately would not necessarily connote failure of the program as a whole or in the long term. Nor would it necessarily be totally successful if all the children did become literate but, despite this, be uninterested in practising their skills; or, in the case of parents, if they lost interest in their children's further progress and literacy achievements; or in the case of teachers, if they wished to have no further involvement with parents in pursuing effective support programs with their children.

The children

As a matter of policy, no child in the program is given a standardised achievement test. Reading ages or performance levels as shown by scaled scores are not sought for two reasons: (i) such measurements say nothing about the process of reading, writing or spelling and, when made, may in any case be misleading about the range of performance levels within which the child functions; (ii) most of the children have been given many standardised tests in the past and have not benefited from them. Under these conditions it is not possible—nor is it considered desirable—to calculate progress or success rates according to pre-program and post-program standardised assessments. Advancements in reading are assessed through progressive Running Records (Clay, 1979) or Miscue Analysis (Goodman and Burke, 1972) and by assessment of the levels of text which children can read and understand. Progress in writing is assessed according to Graves's process writing principles and a particular system of classifying samples of unaided, self-edited writing. Spelling is assessed in the same way. Assessments of children's progress through the program are best made, perhaps, on the basis of the child's functional literacy levels which are judged according to the criteria contained in observation schedules devised especially for the Centre's curriculum (Kemp, in press).

These assessments, however, have to be put into a context of the age (and therefore to some extent the confidence level) of the children entering the program, as well as of their cognitive and functional language capacities. One of the most significant assessments has been the parents' assertions that their children improve markedly because they see their parents as so overtly committed to learning about teaching and to giving them skilled help at home. This factor is, on occasions, so pronounced that one wonders whether the experimental appeal of the program is sufficient to bring about change.

The parents

Attendance and retention rates of parents in the seminar program are over 95%. Perhaps this is an index of the lengths to which parents will go to seek information and, as well, of their capacity to meet the demands made upon them by the seminars. Beyond the seminar program, the parents' commitment to their weekly C.C.A.E. visits, the micro-teaching segments and the regular work schedules at home have been noteworthy.

End-of-seminar program reviews have indicated that the parents work at home with their children on a regular, ten-to-fifteen minutes schedule, varying between three nights a week to six or seven. A few find their time management an insurmountable difficulty: single parents and some of the pair-

systems at home which may best augment the teachers' work at school. These particular literacy teaching efforts have focused upon the schools' corrective functions.

But, given the evidence now available from other sources, it would seem desirable that efforts should also be made by schools to commence such programs either before or simultaneously with young children's entry to school, so that the preventative and enrichment modes of parents' activities in literacy with their children may receive as much attention, at least, as the corrective.

It is our belief that in the program which has been reviewed here, most parents have fulfilled the literacy teaching functions effectively and that with some adaptations the system has application in schools.

References

Governmental Reports Which Have Advocated Parental Involvement
Bullock, A.L.C. *A Language for Life*. Report of Committee of Enquiry into Reading and the Use of Language, London, HMSO, 1975.
Central Advisory Council for Education. *Children and Their Primary Schools* (Plowden Report), London, HMSO, 1967.
House of Representatives Committee. *Report of Inquiry into Learning Disabilities (Cadman Report)*, AGPS 1976.
Warnock, H.M. *Special Educational Needs* Committee of Enquiry into the Education of Handicapped Children and Young People, London, HMSO, 1978.

Parents as Home Literacy Tutors: the British Experience
Jackson, A. and Hannon, P. *The Belfield Reading Project*, Rochdale, Belfield Community Centre, 1981.
Tizard, J., Schofield, W.N. and Hewison, J. "Collaboration Between Teachers and Parents in Assisting Children's Reading", *British Journal of Educational Psychology*, Vol. 52. Part 1, 1982, pp. 1-15.

Parental Involvement in Literacy Learning: the Australian Scene
Amiet, C. and Mackenzie, N. "Parents Participate in New Approaches to Teaching Literacy", *Australian Journal of Reading*, Vol. 8, No. 2, June 1985.
Builder, P. "Involving Parents of Poor Readers", *Australian Journal of Reading*, Vol. 3, No. 4, November 1980.
Builder, P. "Parents as Partners in the Teaching of Reading", *Australian Journal of Reading*, Vol. 5, No. 4, November 1982.
Counsel, M., Mitchell, J. and Portesi, M. "Home Reading: Developing Reading in a Multicultural Setting", in *Reading Around*, Australian Reading Association, No. 1, March 1985.
Fletcher, A., James, T., Cummings, P., Ranking, L. and Napier, L. "The Westfield Experiment" in *The Australian Teacher*, No. 10, 1984.
Richardson, J. and Brown, J. "A Study of Three Methods of Helping Children With Reading Difficulties", *Reading*, Vol. 12, No. 2, 1978, pp. 10-12.

Literacy Learning as Developmental Learning: the Research
Bissex, G. *GNYS at WRK: A Child Learns to Write and Read*, Cambridge, Ma., Harvard University Press, 1980.
Clark, M.M. "What Can We Learn From Them: A Comparison of the Strengths and Weaknesses of Young Fluent Readers and Children with Reading Difficulties", in Burnes, D., Campbell, A. and Jones, R., *Reading, Writing and Multiculturalism*, Adelaide, Australian Reading Association, 1982.
Ferreiro, E. and Teberosky, A. *Literacy Before Schooling*, New Hampshire, Heinemann Educational Books, 1982.

Team Teaching

MARY MANNISON

Brisbane College of Advanced Education
Kelvin Grove

In this chapter team teaching is defined as the simultaneous responsibility by two or more teachers for the total educational program of a group of children. In such a co-operative venture there are benefits for children, parents and teachers. The author describes these benefits, but also stresses that co-operation between teachers requires careful planning and good rapport. A number of case studies of team teaching situations are presented, ranging from the integration of specialist staff into the classroom learning program to the sharing of a large group of children by two teachers in a double-classroom space, employing an "open-plan" approach. The chapter concludes with practical guidelines for teachers interested in trying team teaching. There are ideas for arranging the classroom space, for enlisting the co-operation of parents and children, and for making the most of the team partnership.

Simultaneous responsibility for the total educational program of a group of children.

a team setting, making the therapy an integrated part of the whole educational program. For example, if a handwriting lesson is in progress the physiotherapist may suggest the best posture, the occupational therapist work on appropriate pencil grip, the speech therapist on communication and language related to the activity and the teacher select the next written letter to be practised.

As in any team approach, multi-disciplinary teams need to meet regularly for planning and assessment of their program. The effectiveness of multi-disciplinary teamwork depends on accurate communication of information, ideas and feelings, shared leadership, decision-making by consensus, loyalty (complete compatibility is not vital) to the team, and members having some idea of the dynamics of working in a group (Johnstone, 1980, p. 19, 20). It is also recommended that new teams spend a fair bit of time learning about each other's biases and interests.

C. Bilingual education program teams

"Team teaching in the Northern Territory is a term that is used in Bilingual Schools to describe the way an Aboriginal teacher and a non-Aboriginal teacher work together in the classroom situation" (Graham, 1979, p. 39).

Aboriginal people who speak a language spoken by only a few hundred or at most a thousand people *do* need to learn English, but not merely to gain an education. What is important has to do with what people are "thinking" and with what they do with what they know. In other words, the mother tongue plays a critical role in the achievement of full cognitive development. Graham (1979, p. 29) reviews several studies substantiating this point and concludes also that "great emphasis must be placed on the mother tongue in early years, at least until abstract thinking has taken place, for a child to develop real competency in English when older".

McGill (1981, p. 17) suggests that, in Year 1, 80% of the teaching should be in the Aboriginal language, and that teaching should cover the full range of curriculum subjects. The Northern Territory Department of Education believes that bicultural education is an essential element for significant learning and the maintenance of self-identity and motivation. Aboriginal teachers are a most significant part of bicultural education (Graham, 1981, p. 18).

Two heads are better than one.

to use and carry around with them to guide activities, and is an indicator to parents of what their child is doing.

The team has weekly meetings at which each teacher has an equal input into discussion and decision-making. Children with special problems are discussed and ways to help them formulated.

Teachers on a team are subjected to a large amount of recording, marking, and written descriptions of what they're doing, because everyone on the team needs this information. Deere feels the system could not function without the dedication of teachers; the reward is that they have worked out a way to put the needs and interests of the children first and successfully contribute to the development of their social behaviour and academic ability.

B.   *Gabbinbar Primary School (Queensland)*

There are, of course, many factors that give teachers the idea of team teaching. We have discussed, for example, the non-verbal invitation offered by open-area design. The teachers of Years 1, 2 and 3 at Gabbinbar Primary School were not only in a flexible space unit but, more importantly, wanted to share the same materials. It had been unsatisfactory to shift the *Breakthrough to Literacy* materials from place to place. Planning a permanent (and attractive) setting for the "Sentence Maker", the "Word Makers", "Story Holders" and Breakthrough books brought four teachers together, each with a Year 1-3 family group, to work co-operatively.

One area of their space was set aside for language studies and a co-operative timetable devised, which allowed for two groups at a time to use this space. Consequently, in any given day, up to 120 children may have used the *Breakthrough to Literacy* program (Langdale and McDonald, 1982).

C.   *Maclean Public School (N.S.W.)*

Inspired by discussions of new approaches to teaching, Mathew and Maher (1978) combined their Year 6 classes,

obtained the use of an old assembly hall and set out to try to discover a successful way to combine the traditional with the "open-plan" progressive approach.

The hall was divided into learning areas for maths, reading, craft/art, and group recording, with a central portion left open for whole-group meetings.

The children were put into ability groups for the basic skill areas, and a small school classroom approach was adopted where some groups were given drill, others worked to contract, and both teachers were actively involved in teaching, supervision or giving individual attention to the remedial group. Teaming also aids the learning of basic subjects because the teachers can exchange different techniques and skills.

Contracts are planned and distributed every Friday. The contract and theme approaches help integrate activities in Social Science, and expressive areas of the curriculum, and allow for a great deal of individualised research and selection of learning activities.

The "Square Deal" classroom, according to Mathew and Maher, stimulates bright pupils to extend their work output, motivates the below average pupils to participate in groups, develops self-confidence, affords easy access to use of equipment and materials and encourages co-operation.

Team teaching makes it easier to solve problems, allows teachers to learn from each other, motivates teachers to keep improving their program, relaxes the student-teacher relationship and gives teachers more time to prepare, mark, and record work as they can focus attention on one facet of follow-up.

D.   *Ferny Grove Primary School (Queensland)*

Two teachers who had structured their "egg-crate" classrooms in the manner of the newer flexible-space concepts applied to team teach in the new two-teacher modular unit being built at their school.

The team was sensitive to impressions in the community that children in open classrooms are just "playing around", and

However, you may find discussing or thinking about these questions with a potential team partner a good way to work out your attitudes toward such a venture.

MATERIALS AND EQUIPMENT have to be easy-to-see, accessible, and located where they will be used. Take the doors off the cupboards, label and diagram where things belong.

GROUPING is so much easier in a team. Ability groups are larger and more homogeneous; the work in planning learning centres can be divided in half. Small group work is much more feasible. Give yourselves a break. Take advantage of whole-class instructions whenever you can. As you're not *always* the one who's teaching, you have some extra time, energy, and leftover imagination to plan more interesting presentations.

ATTITUDES TO TEAM TEACHING

Rate each on a scale of five: SA (strongly agree), A (agree), U (undecided), D (disagree), or SD (strongly disagree).

1.	SA	A	U	D	SD	I lack enough information about team teaching to make a decision for or against it.
2.	SA	A	U	D	SD	I think team teaching would provide the best instruction collectively possible.
3.	SA	A	U	D	SD	My time is too limited to explore the possibilities of team teaching.
4.	SA	A	U	D	SD	I am afraid that team teaching may encourage teachers to avoid improvement in their areas of weakness.
5.	SA	A	U	D	SD	Combined with the ideas on a teaching team, my teaching would be more effective.
6.	SA	A	U	D	SD	I plan to remain largely responsible for the instruction of my particular class.
7.	SA	A	U	D	SD	As part of a teaching team, I could spend more time developing creativity, responsibility and habits of inquiry in students.
8.	SA	A	U	D	SD	Team teaching may stifle my creativity in the classroom.
9.	SA	A	U	D	SD	I believe the child benefits more when team teaching is used.
10.	SA	A	U	D	SD	Use of team teaching would allow me to put more varied content into my lessons.
11.	SA	A	U	D	SD	I believe there is an opportunity for teachers ''not to pull their weight'' in team teaching situations.
12.	SA	A	U	D	SD	I can function as well as a member of a teaching team as I can teaching alone.
13.	SA	A	U	D	SD	I would find it very difficult to co-ordinate my teaching with other teachers.
14.	SA	A	U	D	SD	Team teachers with different philosophies than mine would confuse students.
15.	SA	A	U	D	SD	I try to use the best skills of people who can contribute to the learning of my students.
16.	SA	A	U	D	SD	Team teaching would allow me to capitalise on my special interests and abilities.
17.	SA	A	U	D	SD	I imagine team teaching would enhance the professional growth of team members.
18.	SA	A	U	D	SD	I'm not sure I'd like another staff member present while I am teaching.
19.	SA	A	U	D	SD	I think that variety in teaching personalities on a teaching team would increase pupil learning.

Johnstone, Peter. "A multidisciplinary team approach in special education" in *Pivot*, vol. 7, no. 1, pp. 18-20, 1980.

Johnstone, Peter. "A team approach for helping the disabled" in *Education News*, vol. 18, no. 3, pp. 34-37, March, 1983.

Kaminski, Eugene. "Working in a flexible space classroom" in *Journal of the Open Education Association of Queensland*, vol. 2, no. 3, pp. 19-23, Nov., 1978.

Langdale, Owen, and McDonald, Torquil. "How to use a language experience approach and remain sane" in *Reading Techniques, Materials and Organization*, Papers of the Inaugural Conference, Brisbane, 1982, Stewart-Dore, Nea, and Van Homrigh, Pam (Eds), pp. 192-196.

Laslett, Alan. "Open space means change: research and the teacher" in *Opinion*, vol. 8, no. 4, pp. 24-26, Dec., 1979.

Lundin, Roy. "Co-operative planning and teaching" in *S.L.A.N.T. News*, vol. 14, no. 1, pp. 20-25, 1984.

Mathew, Keven, and Maher, Eric. "The square deal way" in *Primary Journal*, no. 3, pp. 50-54, 1978.

McGill, Graham. "Some aspects of education for Aboriginal children in the Northern Territory" in *Australian School Librarian*, vol. 18, no. 1, pp. 15-21, Autumn, 1981.

Miller, I. *Development of an instrument to measure receptivity to educational change amongst primary school teachers* (Masters thesis). Melbourne, Monash University, 1981.

Moeckel, Margot J. "Developing dialogue between teaching-team members in bilingual/bicultural classrooms" in *Aboriginal Child at School*, vol. 10, no. 3, pp. 31-38, June/July, 1982.

Slessar, Michael. "Team teaching: a feasible program for the classroom" in *Idiom*, vol. 18, no. 4, pp. 18-20, 1980.

Sykes, S. "A personal approach to team teaching" in *Inter View*, no. 3, pp. 18-22, 1981.

Warren, Kathie. "Teacher-training sessions for members of the Bilingua Education Program Team" in *Developing Education*, vol. 6, no. 5, pp. 42-44, April, 1979.

Western, Tim. "Rossbourne House—providing a support to the system. A multi-disciplinary approach" in *Australian Journal of Remedial Education*, vol. 13, no. 4, pp. 31-32, 1981.

Learning Centres and Literacy Development

LEN UNSWORTH

This chapter focuses on the use of teacher-made learning centres as a means of fostering independent learning while at the same time providing stimulating "whole language" activities. The author begins by outlining the principles which underlie the effective classroom use of learning centres. He then presents a series of illustrated examples of learning centre activities designed by various teachers. The activities described are drawn specifically from infants classrooms, in order to demonstrate that this approach may be used at all stages of primary education. Means of developing pupils self-evaluation are suggested, and the chapter concludes with a survey of the advantages of this approach.

access to computers, slide/tape and filmstrip machines etc. but much can be done with a listening post and the imaginative use of a simple audio cassette player. Now that meaningless phonic drills and sight word repetitions have been abandoned, the language master can be recycled and used to provide access to interesting tasks for pupils who have difficulty with reading e.g. crossword clues on language master cards.

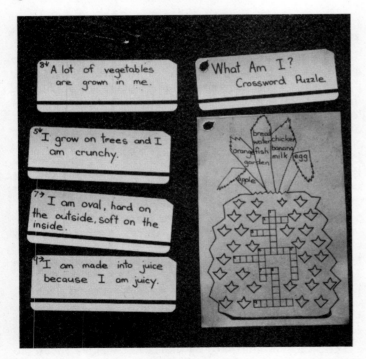

As well as providing multi-media materials, learning centres also provide multi-level activities. This means that all children can undertake the same kind of learning experience but with varying levels of support according to their particular needs.

The crossword clues on the language master is one example, but these cards can also be used to provide access to "cloze" learning tasks for pupils who would have difficulty with conventional print format. Further examples of the ways in which learning tasks can be differentiated according to pupil needs will be dealt with in the descriptions of sample learning centres. One must beware that the use of audio-visual equipment does not imply a predominantly passive role for the learner. For this reason the use of manipulative tasks and a variety of task types is important to maintain the active interest of all pupils.

Independent

One of the major goals for learning centres is to encourage children to be more self-directing in their learning. This implies the opportunity for children to negotiate objectives and to select from a range of tasks and materials. For this to occur the options available at the learning centre must be very clear. They should be discussed with the children and then clearly displayed for future reference. Children need to understand:

* what they can and should do
* how to do it
* when to do it
* where to work
* how and where to obtain materials
* what they should do with completed work
* what they should do when their work is completed
* how they participate in the evaluation process.

Before the learning centre begins actual operation, it is recommended that teachers organise a "rehearsal of procedures" for all pupils. Teachers should first of all explain the use of the centre to all pupils. Groups should then be allowed about five minutes at the centre to familiarise themselves with the layout, procedures etc. If necessary any remaining issues of concern can be clarified with the class. A scheduling device should indicate when particular pupils have access to the centre

The books had been previously read aloud to the class by the teacher and then the taped versions became part of the learning centres for "read along" purposes. Variations to the usual "read along" procedure can assist in maintaining pupils' active interest in a story which they have heard before. For example, with "Gertrude . . ?" the teacher put the overhead projector on the floor near the listening post and provided the children with silhouettes of the main characters so that the children could animate the story with shadow figures as they followed the text.

Stories read in class can be revisited and the children's comprehension consolidated by use of "language master" activities. In the case of "The Three Pigs", the children were given a pack of illustrated language master cards which they were required to sequence and then listen to through the language master to check whether they were sequenced correctly. A similar but more demanding task was set up for the "Gertrude" story. A pack of language master cards contained a precis of the story which the children had to sequence. They then listened to the order of their version on the language master to decide whether any rearrangement was necessary. The compatibility of the small symbols on the reverse side of the cards allowed the teacher (or supervising parent or aide) to see quickly how successful the children were. Many teachers find commercially produced stamps useful for this purpose.

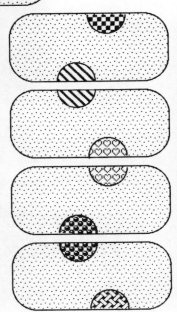

The same principle can be applied to other topics with older children as illustrated in the pupils' "Star Wars" texts. The plastic sleeves allow the texts to be removed and then replaced appropriately by children. The texts can be cut up and children asked to reconstruct them and paste them on a new card. Blue tac can be used to cover selected words with blank cards and children can write the missing words on the plastic sleeve using water-based textas.

R2D2 and C3PO were walking across the sand until they got to Jabba's palace. They had a message for Jabba from Luke.

I broke the eggs into the bowl. After I put the eggs in, I put milk in the bowl.

Class work on the "pirate" included "picture talks" based on overhead transparencies of relevant illustrations from the *Captain Pugwash*. These were later included in the learning centre as part of an activity where children matched them to the appropriate text cards. The previous classroom work "primed" children for success on this learning centre task.

Another method of consolidating children's learning from stories read in class was by use of "sentence wheels". The "sentence wheels" for the "Gertrude" centre were positioned inside a model of her house so that when they were turned one word appeared in the window of the house to provide the "actor" in the sentence:

individual word cards correctly within the clozed text. The constructed book had each page covered with contact so the children could also complete the tasks using water-based textas instead of sentence and word cards.

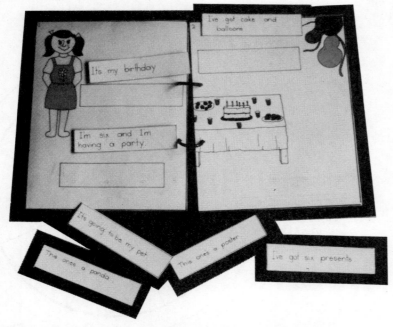

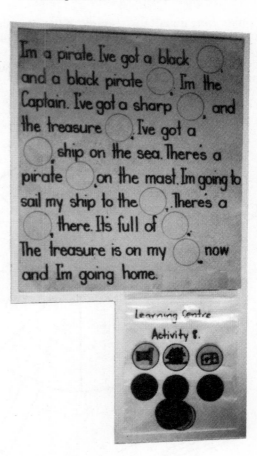

Another novel format for cloze tasks is known as "peg it" cloze. In the "pirate" centre this was set up at two levels of difficulty. At the first level pupils were provided with a circular piece of cardboard from the centre of which radiated various "content units" relevant to the theme e.g. "a pirate", "treasure chest" etc. The teacher had printed common "signalling units" (e.g. "I'm", "That's a", "It's") on wooden clothes pegs which the pupils had to attach to the outside of the card in the appropriate location. The more difficult version had two circular

pieces of card. One was about half the diameter of the other and they were attached at the centre. Radiating from the centre of the smaller circle were, once again, relevant content units but around the edge of the larger circular piece of card were

"Jig-saw Stories" are a means of providing additional cues in text and picture-matching tasks so that success is guaranteed for less able pupils and their text comprehension is further stimulated. In the "pirate" centre pupils had to match pictures with texts and they could choose from texts at three levels of sophistication. The texts on white card were the simplest. These sentences consisted of signalling units and content units. The texts on blue card contained additional "elaborating" units while the most sophisticated texts on the red card contained combinations of elaborating units. If pupils chose the white card they could correctly match each of the texts to the appropriate picture by using the jig-saw cues. They could also do this if they chose to use the blue card but the red card contained no jig-saw cues.

Of course children are not precluded from using combinations of coloured cards to match the pictures and text and complete the story. Children who are able to use some of the red cards but are not confident with all of them could complete the story with simpler cards and in the process clarify their understanding of the remaining red cards. The jig-saw idea was also used in the "Gertrude" and "The Three Pigs" learning centres.

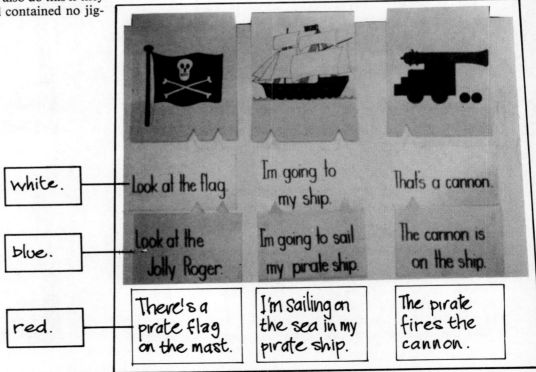

"The Pinballs" learning centre also provided the opportunity for independent research. in this story Harvey has two broken legs and the Benson twins have broken hips. Pupils investigated the formation and function of the bones of the human body.

"What do I do when I'm finished?"

Learning centres should always contain activities which children can go to when they have completed the work undertaken for a particular session. One of the best resources is an abundant supply of additional books related to the focus of the centre. For example, the following were just some of the books which accompanied the "Mouse House":

The Town Mouse and the Country Mouse, illust. by Rene Cloke, Award Publications Ltd., London, 1982.

The Mouse and the Egg, by William Mayne, Julia McRae Books, London, 1980.

Mouse Trouble, by John Yeoman and Quentin Blake, Picture Puffins, Ringwood, Victoria, 1972.

Molly Mouse Goes Shopping, by Carl Koelling, William Collins, Sydney, 1979.

The Kettleship Pirates, by Rodney Peppe, Picture Puffins, Ringwood, Victoria, 1985.

Tim Mouse, by Judy Brook, World's Work Ltd., London, 1982.

The Magnificent Morris Mouse Clubhouse, by Gail Gibbons, Franklin Watts, New York, 1981.

A Number of Mice, by Helen Craig, Aurum Press, London, 1978.

Cats and Mice, by Rita Golden Gelman, Scholastic Book Services, New York, 1978.

Little Mouse on the Prairie, by Stephen Cosgrove, Price Stern Sloan, Los Angeles, 1980.

"The Three Pigs" centre included a board and dice game based on the story, designed for small group use.

The board was clearly marked into 80 numbered squares. On about every eighth square, players would encounter directions

ACTIVITY 5

BROKEN BONES

Directions

In "the Pinballs" by Betsy Byars, Harvey has two broken legs and the Benson twins have broken hips.

* Find out about bones, what they are made of and their job as part of the human body.

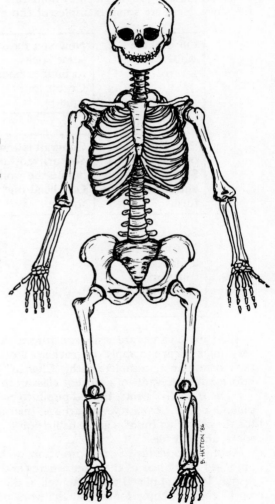

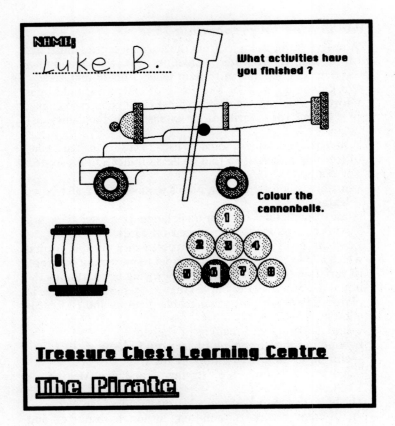

Treasure Chest Learning Centre

The Pirate

Advantages of teacher-made learning centres

* They respond immediately and specifically to the observed needs and interests of the children.
* They reflect the teacher's up-to-date understanding of the processes of literacy development and implications for the classroom.
* They allow the teacher to determine an appropriate, individual diet of traditional and modern children's literature, informational prose, environmental print etc.
* Format variations and original presentation maintain pupil interest in theoretically sound teaching strategies.
* They facilitate the integration of a range of materials (perhaps over several curriculum areas) from diverse and multi-media sources, around teacher/pupil-negotiated learning experiences.
* They provide self-directing and (semi) self-evaluating learning experiences which avoid the mechanical, multiple choice, or repetitious approach of much commercially produced material.
* They provide a model of the kinds of learning processes and products which are valued in the classroom.
* They allow instructions and other stimulus materials to be personalised through inclusion of individual student's names, reference to their interests, home, friends, school acquaintances and activities.

Bibliography

Byars, B. *The Pinballs*, London: Macmillan Education, 1977.

Dr. Seuss. *Green Eggs and Ham*, London: Collins, 1962.

Galdone, J. and Galdone, P. *Gertrude the Goose Who Forgot*, New York: Watts, 1975.

Hart, N. and Walker, R. et al. *The Mount Gravatt Reading Series Level I*, Sydney: Addison Wesley, 1977.

Ingram, B., Jones, N. and Butt, M. *The Workshop Approach to Classroom Learning Centres*, New York: Park, 1975.

Lewis, C.S. *The Lion, The Witch and the Wardrobe*, London: Goeffrey Bles, 1950.

Peppe, R. *The Mice Who Lived in a Shoe*, Melbourne: Puffin, Penguin Books Australia Ltd., 1981.

Petreshene, S. *The Complete Guide to Learning Centres*, Palo Alto, California: Pendragon, 1978.

Ross, T. *The Three Pigs*, London: Andersen Press, 1983.

Ryan, T. *Captain Pugwash*, London: Bodley Head, 1957.

Thompson, R. and Merritt, K. Turn on to a learning centre. *The Reading Teacher*, 28, 384-88, 1975.

Waynant, F. and Wilson, R. *Learning Centres: A Guide For Effective Use*, Pennsylvania: McGraw-Hill, 1974.

Waynant, F. and Wilson, R. *Learning Centres II: Practical Ideas for You*, Pennsylvania, McGraw-Hill, 1977.

Williams, G. Literature and the development of interpersonal understanding. In Unsworth, L. (Ed.), *Reading: An Australian Perspective*, Melbourne: Nelson, 1985.

Some of the photographs of learning centre materials submitted for this chapter were not of reproducible quality. Therefore a number of teacher-drawn activities and evaluation sheets have been redrawn on the Macintosh Macdraft computer program. Teachers with an interest in computers may wish to experiment with various graphics programs themselves. For those with access to the Macintosh, Macpaint and Macdraw are other suitable programs. PETA wishes to thank Mr. George Wilkie for his assistance in the production of graphics for this chapter.